Terry C. Holdbrooks, Jr.

Disclaimer: All names except the prisoners' and Terry Holdbrooks' have been changed to protect the safety and security of those soldiers still serving in the armed forces. Some individuals with names attributed to them are in fact combinations of different nameless soldiers who shared common characteristics.

ISBN 10: 1481849131

ISBN 13: 978-1481849135

LCCN: 2013908287

CreateSpace Independent Publishing Platform

North Charleston, SC

Table of Contents

Foreword

مثل الاسلام كشجرة جميلة عطرة بهيجة الالوان التي بنموها يستفيد كثير من
تخيل الان لو ان هذه من ظلها ثمارها رائحتها الفريدة والوانها الممتعة الناس
الشجرة كلما بدأت بالنمو خربت او اقتلعت من جذورها؟أو أن الناس نهوا عن
الاقتراب منها أو قيل لهم انها مضرة سامة وانهم سيهلكون ان فعلوا ذلك؟سصدقون
الاشاعة دون ان يتأكدوا من مدى صحتها ويبتعدون عن هذه الشجرة الطيبة و
بالرغم من ذلك كان هناك يحرمون من منافعها طالما تمسكوا بتلك النظرة عنها
جندي يعرف باسم هولدبروكس على وشك ان يسمع عن هذه الشجرة ويسأل عنها
في أسوأ الاماكن على وجه الارض حيث لا تنمو سوى اشجار الكراهية وينتشر
بذلات السجناء البرتقالية و العداء بين الناس ..هذا المكان الملقب بخليج غوانتنام
اغلالهم لم تمنع هولدبروكس من ان يتقرب منهم و يتناقش معهم حول الاسلام كان
شجاعا في طرحه و اسئلته لقد اندهشت من آرائه الحرة(المختلفة عن آرائي) من
منطقه وذهنه الصافي الذي لم يكن مشوشا بالدعايات الخاطئة و الاحكام المسبقة
الغرور و حب السيطرة على السجناء لم تتحكم فيه مثل باقي الجنود الآخرين
...بدلا من ذلك نشأ كارها للاذى و التعسف لانه رأى ما لم يره زملاؤه و اكتشف
ما لم يكتشفوه ... أصر على المضي قدما في بحثه عن الشجرة بعد ان احب
وصفها ورأى تأثيرها على السجناء أراد امتلاك الشجرة و خدمتها ...تلك هي
السعادة التي تغمر الانسان العاصي التائه في دنيا الذنوب لما يعلم ان الله الكريم
الغفور الودود في انتظار عودته وتوبته

"The example of Islam is like that of a beautifully-scented, colorful tree because when grown it develops many things that people come to benefit from like shade, fruit, unique scents and beautiful colors to enjoy. Now imagine if this tree, every time it began to grow, was crushed and uprooted, and people were told to be careful of it, for it was a harmful, poisonous tree and if it grew it would even destroy them from its poisonous essence; eventually people would grow accustomed to staying away from it without seeing its beauty or benefits, and those who lost out would lose out, and the ones who stay away would never come back to the tree's beauty. However, a soldier known as Holdbrooks was to hear about this tree, and to ask for its benefits in the worst of places, where no tree or plant ever grows, only hostility and hatred between people, in a place called Guantanamo Bay. The prisoners' orange suits and chains did not stop Holdbrooks from becoming close to the prisoners and discussing Islam with them. He was brave in his approaches, in his questioning; I was amazed by his free mind, which was not like mine, his logic, and clear mind was not confused with false claims and prejudices. The arrogance and love of power over prisoners did not overtake him like it overtook many other soldiers; instead he grew to detest the abuses, for he saw what his other colleagues didn't see, and found what the other guards didn't find, and he was adamant to continue his search because he loved the description of the tree, and saw its effect amongst the prisoners, he wanted to own the tree, and wanted the tree to own him. It is the happiness that overcomes the sinful lost servant when he finds the forgiving, kind Lord waiting for him."

Ahmed Errachidi (Formerly Detainee 590 – "The General")

Traitor?

The Greatest Tragedy

Of all places to have a tickle of laughter in my throat, this was most inappropriate. For all intents and purposes, I should have been very somber, very sad and very angry. This was, I now know, the expected mood. On a sunny day in June, standing in front of the two-year old ruins at the World Trade Center in New York City, with my fellow soldiers standing all around me, I let out a small laugh. In my defense, something I had just read was cause for amusement. It was also something that set the tone for my time at Guantanamo Bay, Cuba (GTMO).

'This is the greatest tragedy to happen to all of mankind.'

This sentence was scrawled on the wall where citizens wrote quotations or words of condolence, or listed the names of family members that had been lost in the attack. At this point, all members of my company were standing quietly in our civilian clothes, somberly reading the comments other Americans had left on the wall. This visit was part of the 'training' we received in preparation for our time at GTMO. Upon reading it I pointed, chuckled, and declared: "This wasn't even close to the worst tragedy to happen to mankind!" I expected at least some smiles, perhaps a nod and maybe even a fellow chuckler.

On the contrary, every eye narrowed; someone even hissed. My bemused reaction to the statement obviously was not shared. Feeling the need to explain myself further, I remarked how incredibly ignorant the writer was of history, of wars and of genocides, of oppression by any dominant regime. The author of that comment, declaring the attack of 9/11 to be the greatest tragedy, revealed a thorough lack of awareness of contemporary history. My explanation met with neither understanding nor change in attitude. Blank, angry stares, admonishment and a question about my allegiance all followed my futile attempt at a history lesson.

"Remember, these are not people! These are hate-filled, evil, terrorist dirt farmers, and they will stop at nothing to kill you! NEVER FORGET THIS! NEVER FORGET 9/11!

NEVER FORGET WHY WE ARE FIGHTING!" my superior officers decried.

Their position clarified, I was roundly chastised for expressing my view about the certain tragedy in New York City. I realized then and there that my career in the military was not going to be demonstrated, as I had assumed, by becoming a better American citizen. It was not going to be found in improving the lives of my fellow citizens. It was going to manifest itself in being at war with strangers from across the sea and sand, considering them as enemies while knowing nothing about them, and 'getting back' at them for a crime that was ascribed to them without substantial evidence. I did not take to heart their defamations then but kept it under advisement; I did learn to keep my 'liberal' opinions to myself, and to toe the line. It was part of the training, and a part of the routine of every single day during my time at GTMO—to be reminded of this message of retaliation. It was very important to my senior officers that those under their charge never forget about the World Trade Center's destruction and the demise of its occupants. Their calumny was squared against me (of all people) since the actual event, when it occurred, was to me just another news anecdote, blown out of proportion by the media.

Prior to September 2001, I recall there weren't as many American-flag bumper stickers, nor vocal patriots, nor 'Support our Troops' propaganda in the United States as were apparent after that date. I recall with wonder the fuss made about 9/11. I had come home late from an evening of playing pool and drinking with friends, and just wanted to go to bed. Before the effects of the evening had worn off, my grandmother woke me to come watch the news on TV.

"Who cares, let me sleep please," I replied. However, in my grandparents' home, where watching the news was done more religiously than attending church and special news reports warranted vigils, I was not allowed the comfort of my bed. I sat in front of the TV beside my grandmother, watching the same footage over and over and over: boom!...boom!...boom!...the plane hitting the first tower on repeat. "Well, this is really fascinating, but I would like to go back to bed now for a little while," I commented, returning to my room. Within moments of lying back down, the second tower was hit.

She woke me up a second time, and I then had to endure some of the most ridiculous noise that I had ever heard come from the news channels.

'This is the end of the world!', 'This is the beginning of World War Three!' and even 'Aliens have taken control of our planes and are diverting them into towers!' were some of the incredible commentary allotted for newscasters nationally. Again, I thought to myself: *no big deal, it was two planes. Oh, well.* The news media were always reporting about some kind of violent attack. Annoyed by the hysteria and the bizarre conclusions of the news media—shooting in the deep dark about the reasons or motivations of the attackers of the World Trade Center—I shut off every TV in the house.

For the rest of that day and those following, I tried in vain to escape the 'news' of the attacks. However, anyone who can remember that day clearly must recall how nearly impossible it was to avoid the media's unconditional immersion in it. Stopping first at a local coffee shop, I saw that the news was playing on all three televisions, prompting all in the shop to discuss it incessantly. I then moved on to have some work done on my truck; the only television in the waiting room had the same footage playing repeatedly, accompanied by the same random, ludicrous guessing as to the cause.

A friend from school came to mind as a place where I could escape the hype, but I found this friend similarly glued to his TV along with four other friends.

"What is wrong with the world today? Don't you people want to do anything else aside from watch this crap over and over?" I exclaimed. They did not budge. It wasn't the first time I had expressed a unique position on world events, and it would certainly not be the last. Raised in my grandparents' home, I had held the understanding that the news was supposed to report what happened based on concrete evidence, not based on speculation, hyperbole, or theory. This treatment of the destruction of the World Trade Center by the news media afforded me a lesson in truth: America is inviolable, except when it's not.

I considered a scene from the movie *SLC Punk* in which the two protagonists are sitting in front of an inoperative television with a photo of Ronald Reagan taped to the front. That was what I felt was going on: there was an actor on the television, nothing more.

Given my personal response to the attacks on 9/11, I felt clear about my motivation in enlisting in the armed forces: unlike many others enlisting at the time, my decision was not bolstered by a vengeful feeling about the events of 9/11. I believed that the Army training would give me a purpose in life, and possibly bring my family legacy out of the Arizona dust. Although full of energy, youth has with it the need for direction. My upbringing had not instilled in me a sense of structure or order, but I did have a sense of duty to my country and a desire to make it a better place. In search of guidance and personal development, the idea of enlisting resonated. I decided to sign up in an attempt to 'be-all-I-could-be'.

Michael Moore's film *Fahrenheit 9/11* demonstrates that U.S. Military recruiters are more aggressive now than in the past. The fact that I had to hound recruiters in order to enlist in the Army should surprise anyone who has lived in the United States post-9/11. It was for the simple reason that the War on Terror was still in its early phases; not as many American soldiers had died yet or, in other words, needed replacing.

Perhaps the recruiters noticed my slight stature and thought that I wouldn't last long in the Army. It may have been my tattoos and the multiple piercing in my ears. At that time, Army recruiters had the luxury of being fussy and waiting for what they considered was their ideal recruit. However, my persistence paid off, and after four weeks I was able to enlist in August of 2002.

They began the paperwork, which included research into my tattoos to make sure they were not gang related. The designs and patterns were of my personal choice. I held no ties to gangs: I paid for the ink impressions in order to communicate about myself to whoever saw them. Medical screenings and testing then took place to ensure that I could enlist and serve. Although slight in stature, they found I was physically fit.

Due to my results from the ASVAB test, I had a wide variety of choices from which to choose an occupation. My foolish question, "Which jobs are giving a bonus?" steered me towards military police work. Had I known what the job actually entailed, I would have chosen differently, but I was beguiled by the lure of material rewards and how the Army sold it to me. I discovered later that being a military police officer would not allow me to be in combat or see 'action', which was disappointing. It would instead deliver me to a grim place called Guantanamo Bay, Cuba.

Although it was good for my resume, military police work involved many monotonous tasks. I was desperately craving a sense of order and structure to my life, plus some excitement and world travel. I hoped to learn new ways of life and experience different cultures. However, my work involved policing those who were supposed to be policing the United States. I soon realized I had chosen the most unimaginably boring job. While military police work did nothing at the time to expand my awareness through knowing other cultures and seeing faraway places, I would soon be able to experience all of this, albeit figuratively, working at GTMO.

Eventually the day came to go to Basic Training. I woke up early, about 0400, my recruiter picking me up at 0530. Dropping me off at the airport, he gave me a packet and said, "Your plane leaves at 0800. Have a safe flight. Good luck, Private."

I smoked what I thought might be my last cigarette for a long while, and then went undeterred through airport security. I settled into my seat on the plane headed for Fort Leonard Wood in Missouri and waited to see what they had planned for me. I imagined myself at the time to be among the defenders of America, the best of the best, to become a role model for and a leader of society. I hoped to become a diplomat for American culture. I hoped all-I-could-be would be enough to bring to my life the changes that would make my existence worthwhile and beneficial to my country and possibly the world.

In the Army Now

Arriving at a duty station such as Ft. Leonard Wood for Basic Training, one doesn't just jump right in. At the in-processing centers, known as reception battalions, privates learn their first and most important lesson in government work: hurry up and wait. Those participating in any aspect of American government must hurry and deliver the desired results to the expectant, and then the expectant will take their sweet time delivering to the party what they had hoped to gain. My entire experience with the government revolved around this idea. I hurried to do what I was told, performed the tasks expeditiously, and was forced to wait some time for the response. Anyone familiar with government can recognize the concept.

For perhaps four or five days straight I received shots, haircuts, clothing and physical testing. Nearly five-hundred clueless recruits were harried along by drill-sergeants-in-training running the facility. It made for a slow process. It instilled in me and others a great desire to begin the real Basic Training, which began with a ride in a cattle cart. Shoved in there with about fifty others and our bags, I arrived at my unit: E Company 787th Military Police Battalion.

Most people who have only experienced the military through movies and television shows have a glamorized picture of Basic Training. Movies generally depict sergeants hitting and using profanity on their trainees, making them train until they pass out from exhaustion. Hollywood tries to make it look tough and so do the documentaries about America's military. I was actually excited at the prospect of being pushed to my limit, but was disappointed as basic training proved rather easy. It was less difficult than working at a fast-food restaurant.

There were ropes to climb up and repel down, areas to crawl in, obstacle courses to negotiate, and adult-sized jungle gyms to conquer. There were set schedules for mealtimes, classes and lights-out. Basic Training was a gentle joke, especially for someone who craved the organized simplicity.

Basic Training also consisted of going to the firing range and shooting weapons to which I had never before had access. Along with learning to use them, I was also taught how to clean and repair the weapons. I was taught the use, repair and upkeep of the vehicles used on base, and the details of my MOS (the military police work in which I received training). The rest of basic training was like summer camp, minus the weenie-roasts. I loved the weapons training and had a knack for it, qualifying as expert with little effort. I had a special talent for skill shooting and welcomed the physical conditioning, as I loved to feel in shape. The confidence courses and physical endurance courses were like going to the playground as a child, and the classes were so simple that anyone could have passed them. I thrived on the structure and order of this time in the military; I felt as though it was a fine life—exactly what I needed. In addition, the food was great: the chow hall always seemed to have a variety of tasty items from which to choose. With the range of healthy choices, it wasn't hard for me to clean each plate.

The structure of having set rules and everyone around me following them created a safe and secure place, unlike anything I had ever experienced. My life growing up was not as hard as some others might have had, but it did lack structure and even my parents refused to follow many of society's rules. I felt in the military—in Basic Training—that I had found my place in the world, one where everything was orderly, made sense and was in line with the kind of great citizen I was expecting to be. It was where we were upholding the Constitution and helping further the cause of the United States in bringing democracy and fairness to the world. I felt that this training and conditioning could not help but create people who would excel in society, no matter where they were stationed. I would not know until later how misplaced my trust in the system was: I trusted the people and the system, when perhaps only the system deserved that honor.

Off-barracks, we had little more than two strip clubs and a Wal-Mart. People go to St. Robert, Missouri, the gateway of Ft. Leonard Wood, for two reasons (generally): to die or to buy methamphetamine, as the town is a production capital of the drug.

It was a hell on earth, filled with backwards racists and small-town hicks who inhabited trailer parks. My interaction off base was held almost exclusively at a Waffle House in St. Robert.

So Ft. Leonard Wood was where life took place for me. I had some of the greatest drill sergeants that I would ever meet: SFC Oakes, SSG Ellis, and SSG Payne. I developed great relationships with them, and stayed in touch with them throughout my entire stint in the Army. These three sergeants were a constant inspiration to me. They taught me some important life skills that I had not been taught by my father: discipline, respect and putting anger to constructive uses. Oakes, the Senior Drill Instructor, was what we referred to as 'high speed'. He was like a Sapper, Ranger, and Special Forces all rolled into one. Ellis was laid back. He sang songs when we marched, and sat back and watched as everything happened. But when it came time, he would be six feet in a private's rear quarters if they screwed up. My favorite by far was Payne. He had a great deal of wisdom and intelligence, and tried to share them with those who were willing to hear him. I enjoyed the few times I was able to just sit and talk with Payne, one human to another, no military involved. It felt good to be treated like that by a drill sergeant, and it wasn't the only time that I had that experience with certain leaders during my time in the Army.

Told by friends who had been in the military before me that Basic Training would take forever, I was surprised to find that time sped by. It was no time at all until I had just two weeks left before graduation.

Obviously, physical fitness is a large part of qualifying for military service, and while I had been admitted by recruiters, could run for miles and found push-ups easy enough, the big worry for me was the sit-ups. For the physical training test, we had to perform a minimum of fifty-three sit-ups, which were timed, as part of the requirements to graduate. It kept me up late at night with worry that my slight frame wouldn't be able to pull through for me, and I'd be sent back to Basic Training until I was able. After fifteen, I tired; at twenty, I became exhausted. By thirty-five or forty, I felt as though my abdominal muscles would cease to listen to my brain. Every single time it was a struggle. I really didn't want to be 'that guy' that was resorted back into Basic Training while the rest of those around me graduated on to the real Army. As with other things in life that people wait for, dreading, the time came earlier than I wanted. I began the sit-ups as I had always done before, and it was as if my body went into autopilot: exhausted after having pushed my body to its limit, my abdomen must have called in reserve energy from my brain, as I didn't recall that last sit-up.

When I regained consciousness, I questioned as to whether or not I had made it and got back the incredible answer: "Yes."

This meant, of course, that it was graduation time. A great part of my joy at passing the different tests Basic Training offered me was to see my grandfather in attendance at the graduation ceremony. Having served in the military as a merchant marine, my grandfather attended the graduation ceremony of his grandson as a father would have. Following a family tradition of military accomplishment made me feel good about myself, and good about the world. I felt proud, as if I'd finally done something that went beyond the simple skills I'd learned from my parents. I felt I had excelled, meeting the primary goal for which I had been striving when enlisting. It was a day to remember: I threw my hat in the air, ate cake, hugged my grandfather, smiled and celebrated without any knowledge or care as to where or when I would be deployed during that tense, post 9/11 wartime.

The aforementioned Waffle House was the only off-of-base location in which I felt comfortable. It was in essence a sort of home for me, as I returned to it at different points in my life. I sat there lonely on holidays, drinking coffee or smoking, reflecting quietly on life and the world I lived in. It was also a place in which I would occasionally sober up on the way back to the base after a night of drinking. The night of graduation, I sat there with my grandfather and smoked my first cigarette in 18 weeks (with the capacity to only finish half a butt). Soon I learned where I would be stationed.

Out of 146 trainees, I was the only one who was stuck staying at Ft. Leonard Wood. Any ideas I had entertained of exotic or exciting duty stations were undercut by the news that I'd be staying in good old Missouri. It was a real downer for me—especially given that I was the only one chosen to stay. It wasn't because I'd been singled out in some type of disciplinary action, although to me it sure felt like it. I took it as an omen of things to come, an omen that told me I was the black sheep of the flock. I was among the most miserable of the graduates as I flew back home to Arizona for a couple of weeks to let the news sink in.

When I came back and saw all of my high school friends again, it was amazing, especially the second evening back. I met a friend at the local diner who had brought along a female friend of his. She was the most beautiful woman I had ever seen; I couldn't take my eyes off of her. The first time she spoke to me, I felt my jaw drop a little and I was speechless.

"Nice red pants," she said, in a slightly mocking tone. Unfamiliar with the way some women express interest in a guy, I was instantly annoyed with her.

She may have been interested in me at that first meeting or perhaps just unsure what to make of me. As we ate, we made small talk about our lives, her about her cell phone bill and me about Basic Training. Then she broke off from that.

"Do you ever shut up?" she asked.

"Do you always wear so much makeup?" I replied. Then, silence. That set an awkward tone for the rest of the evening, making me feel sure that she did not like me at all. We bickered back and forth the rest of the evening in a light, bantering way. Those accompanying us that evening were given the impression we couldn't stand each other, but of course, that was the point. We didn't want to be set up by friends, but to explore through sarcasm and wit whether or not we could become a pair. When I got home, I could not stop thinking about her, and hoped that this beautiful woman with the gorgeous hair had some interest in me, despite first impressions. After that evening, I was in love.

My hopes were soon realized, as she agreed to come out the next night with our mutual friend and meet me at a pool hall. This time we allowed ourselves to be playful and nicer to each other, our interest in each other now apparent. The two of us ended up under a pool table, talking with each other about everything and anything. I tried on her shoe, her hat. Laughing at my silliness, she fell in love.

Plans were made for another night, and we played it cool with each other and got along well as friends. An unspoken commitment was made, and for the remainder of my two weeks in Arizona we were inseparable. My mother liked her, my siblings liked her; it was as if everything was falling into place. In that small amount of time, she had secured a permanent place in my heart. When the time came to leave, my grandfather picked me up from her home and drove me to the airport, delivering me back to Ft. Leonard Wood with a smile on my face that stretched from ear to ear.

With my faith secured not only in the military system into which I had entered, but in humanity itself and my place in the world through this new relationship, I was ready to be-all-I could-be—for the world and for the woman I loved. I felt sure that wherever I was stationed and whatever trials I faced, my trust in the military and in love would see me through.

Inadequate Training

My assigned duty station was the 252nd Military Police unit. I served as a cop who stayed on the base and took care of the police work. We were a garrison unit. Our co-existence with the 463rd had resulted in a sibling nomenclature within the Army's protocols in which ours was designated 'sister', theirs 'brother'—the implied subtext of which was demeaning. Whereas our unit stayed on the base and patrolled—dealing with mundane civil affairs and enjoying a cushy military life—the 463rd was 'FORSCOM', deploying, fighting wars and shooting terrorists: a 'real' Army unit. An example of the type of guy that was in that unit was Sgt. Johnsville, who I had the misfortune to encounter later at GTMO. However, at this time—prior to meeting him and his ilk—I felt envy for that 'real' Army lifestyle.

Most of the time we would be discharging our assigned duties: protecting and working the four or five gates on Fort Leonard Wood. About as challenging as cutting butter, the work included duties like checking ID's and vehicles to ensure that everyone who was coming in had a reason and purpose to be on base that did not include blowing it up. It was monotonous, but for someone fresh out of Basic Training, it was all I knew of military life. Monday through Friday, each day began at 0630 for PT, a ritual I sometimes skipped. I wasn't missed and my absence went unnoticed for some time. Eventually other men who lived in the barracks were blamed for not waking me up. Officially (not ideally), what should have happened is this: my first sergeant should have been upset, in turn upsetting my platoon sergeant., upsetting my squad leader, upsetting my team leader—resulting in me being destroyed. This illustrates how flawed the unit was when I was a part of it. It was the first time I saw that my beloved military (with its rules) worked when everyone was on board with the protocol; when that was breached, the structure dissolved, and rules, along with people, fell through the cracks.

One strange character I met at this time who would follow me throughout my time in the Army, was SFC Neffer. He would blame people for the oddest things, such as my absence from physical training. While he hadn't noticed my absence for nearly two weeks, he finally approached my friend, PFC Malde, and demanded "Where in the hell is that Holdbrooks at, MMMAAALLLLDDDEEEEE!?" The question was strange, given Pvt. Malde didn't live with me or even on my floor in the barracks. SFC Neffer had this interesting swagger: he would sort of strut around when he walked and as he spoke—he was characteristically short and to the point—and K.I.S.S. (keep-it-simple-stupid) was ever present in his speech.

In the 252nd, soldiers came and went as they pleased; the work was robotic and mundane. We worked the road, being essentially police officers. Occasionally we found a drunken driver or something more exciting, like a speeder! A drunken dispute occasionally occurred in the night in a barrack or home, but that was uncommon as well. No one ever really bothered to use the East or West Gates, preferring the North and South instead, with most of the traffic traveling through the former. I did not do too much in (or learn too much about) the real Army during this time.

A highlight of that period was the infatuation and excitement found in my new love interest. My female friend and I would sit and speak for hours each night on the phone, talking to each other about our days and future aspirations and dreams. Developing a long-distance relationship was taxing on us, so I soon felt a visit was in order. It wasn't what you would call 'approved' as no paperwork had been filed, nor signatures signed. Since it was a three-day weekend, I didn't see the harm in leaving as I didn't think I would be missed. So, after a thrilling two months of working on the base trying to manage a relationship with my charming friend, I returned home to see her. We spent the entire weekend together enjoying each other's company, but all too soon the time came to leave again.

On the morning that I was to fly back to Ft. Leonard Wood, we stopped at a McDonald's and shared a goodbye breakfast. I ordered a sausage biscuit; she got pancakes. We sat together and enjoyed that perfect comfortable silence that couples do. The moment was at the same time goofy, passionate and wonderful and was a celebration of the strange and magic little world that she and I, like all new young couples, shared. We were young, dumb, and in love with each other: poised at the precipice to fulfill the American dream. The occasion was neither romantic nor planned, and did not involve me getting down on one knee holding a ring in a precious box.

In between bites of my sandwich, I asked her, "Will you marry me?" She giggled with pieces of pancake in her mouth, swallowed and replied:

"Terry, are you serious? Yes, I'll marry you...if you're serious." We locked eyes, and in a rare moment of seriousness I replied.

"Alright Mrs. Holdbrooks, I'll take that as 'I do'."

I was so happy with her reply. I spent the entire flight home thinking about our wedding and what life would be like with her by my side every day; the family we would start and the home we would build. I thought about the great career ahead of me that would provide for us both. Very much in love, I delighted in just how wonderful she was in every way. When I got off the airplane and met my friends at the terminal, I told them the news. On the way home, while still in the city, we stopped so I could secure a wedding ring. I found and purchased an engagement/wedding ring set at Kay Jewelers of which I was fond.

It was about a month later that she gave up her entire life for me; she moved to Ft. Leonard Wood, leaving her family, friends and career. On a lunch break, we went to the courthouse twenty-nine miles away from the base and were married. On the way home we stopped for coffee and locked ourselves out of her car. It was raining. While anything that happens on your wedding day can be taken as an omen (good or bad), her interpretation of events caused her to express what would become a prophetic statement: "We're certainly not starting off well."

However, we were in love, and as fresh new love is stubborn and unstoppable, we were, for that time, happy. I felt she would be the main pillar of support in my life, the foundation for my work during my time in the Army. I considered that I would support her as well, but did not realize then how her presence in my life and heart would support me too. Our relationship cast light on certain realities for me, and was the one thing among all crazy, dark and jaded things that would shine for me and give me hope in the American dream.

My friends all loved her and she got along with them very well. We started to make a home together and the pieces of life were falling into place. I felt that maybe—at long last—the order and organization in my life was improving my intimate relations too, in welcome contrast to my childhood.

One day in April 2003, PFC Ladd and I were working at the South Gate when SFC Neffer arrived. It was unusual for him to visit during the workday. A Humvee rolled down the road, and out popped Neffer to tell my friend and me that we were being reassigned.

"Holdbrooks, you're going to the 463rd tomorrow. Ladd, you're starting at the Chemical Defense Training Facility," he barked at us, visibly upset.

"Um, why is that SFC Neffer?" I asked.

"Look: you are going, I am going—a bunch of us are going. Just show up for formation tomorrow at 0630 and be ready," he explained. After work that day, I came to the understanding that we were going to the 463rd because the unit had an upcoming deployment and needed soldiers to fulfill the mission requirements. It wasn't for a few more days that I would find out we were meant to work at GTMO.

I enjoyed this unit much more, it being a FORSCOM unit, meaning that we deployed: we were real Army. There was proper structure and proper military bearing. It was like Basic Training again, but at the same time more interesting and lax. People treated each other as soldiers rather than trainees. I adapted quickly to the new environment as it challenged me the way I hoped the Army would. Among the differences I enjoyed the most were that we worked hard, and that I was learning something new every day. We did real training and worked real hours: I had left preschool for high school all in one day. One of the most fun parts of my life were the three years I spent in the 463rd, despite the desolate location in which I spent the later part of my time. I established some lifelong friends quickly upon my arrival. Friendships gained during life in the Army cement quickly through shared experiences and trials. I clicked with another young soldier like myself named PFC Bradley. We became best friends overnight, as we had so much in common: both of us had just recently been married, been through Basic Training and were both wet behind the ears. We had similar tastes in just about everything; we just plain got along. Bradley would serve to be a second pillar that would help get me through my time in the Army.

SFC Jergins was my platoon sergeant in the 463rd, and Sgt. Brassel was my team leader at first. It quickly became clear that this was an entirely different style of company. They trained hard, they worked hard, and I realized what the real Army was like with them. There was always work to be done and sometimes we would be working 12 to 18-hour days: we stayed until the job was done. That's just how the Army is supposed to function; it is very effective when all follow the rules. I enjoyed this company and its pace. They had a platoon which was deployed to Qatar when I arrived, but I don't recall ever having met many '1st platoon' as our schedules were just never coordinated.

I had just gotten into the rhythm of my new unit when I got word that we were going to GTMO. My first thought was: *GTMO? What the hell is that?* GTMO hadn't been in the news yet; it wouldn't be until 2006 that the U.S. government admitted they were keeping prisoners there. Then a second thought came to my mind: *Oh no, what's going to happen to my wife?* This was still April or May, 2003—we had only just married. Now I was scheduled to leave in June for a year to serve and protect our country.

My immediate response was not: *I should Google this place, and learn what is going to happen to me*. Rather, I thought: *I have to tell her, and I have to spend as much time as I can with her before I go*. So that is exactly what I did. I spent the remainder of time I had left with her; hoping to establish a bond strong enough to withstand our separation through my deployment, naively thinking that a lot of bonding in just a few days would be enough. I honestly believed I would have a wonderful wife and a home to come back to if I devoted this short time to her alone. She was upset and worried at first. Her fear and mine (as well as that of many other soldiers) dissipated as the Army began offering us incrementally more information. I dearly wanted to remain with her, but the time came when I had to say goodbye. I left for work that day just like any other, kissing her on the forehead, ending a short and sweet chapter of our new marriage, and beginning a long and arduous chapter of my new military career.

My training and work experience up to June 2003, was of little to no benefit in my upcoming deployment, although perhaps MPs might have come in handy at GTMO to police those out-of-line on base. After leaving Fort Leonard Wood, I headed for Fort Dix, New Jersey, for a conversion course to learn about how to work in a correctional facility. We would only be given two short weeks to learn about how to conduct ourselves in every possible situation that could arise in an entirely different line of work.

Our training at Ft. Dix involved a mock prison, with fellow soldiers playing the part of prisoners and correctional officers of the same rank as us acting as trainers. While it was of course new, those who were training us to work at GTMO had never actually been to Cuba.

We were training inside an imitation prison which fell far short of being anywhere near that of the genuine article. To be fair, however, GTMO is unlike any other prison in the United States. GTMO is nothing like Leavenworth.

However, as the Army trains people to follow orders and to not ask questions, we went through the training. I was still unaware of the realities of GTMO and entirely ignorant of the people I would be guarding, including their language and culture. There was no instruction on Middle Eastern culture or the religion of Islam; we were shown nothing of the actual individuals we would be guarding, their culture or social customs. We just played the clock until our departure.

On the bright side, I met my squad leader, SSG Johnsonville, and my new team leader, Sgt. Green. I was able to get along with these two quite well. Johnsonville had the luxury of having the Army career that I wanted: he had been to Germany, seen some combat, taken some advanced training and was an all-around nice guy. He took to me quickly; I would not interact with even my team leaders in the way he and I would joke around and talk. Sgt. Green was infantry at first, and then became an MP. In fact, he was expert infantry and he had seen some real Army. This is right where I needed to be—under the leadership of some people who knew what they were doing, and had some genuine experience. Others in our squad, such as Sgt. Nord were "high-speed" and freely shared some helpful knowledge—which I lapped up at every opportunity.

However, it was at this time that I began hearing things that would foreshadow the overall atmosphere there. Epithets like 'towel-head', 'camel-jockey', 'sand-nigger' and 'dirt-farmer' began to enter the casual conversation among those in my platoon. 'Taliban', 'Al-Qaeda', 'worst-of-the-worst' and 'extremist' started to get thrown around. I started noticing that more people were making asinine statements like, 'We should just turn that whole part of the world into a big parking lot', or 'We should just bomb all them towel-heads and get out of the Middle East'. This type of conversation started at about the same time that the indoctrination and reprogramming began. Its purpose was to lead us to feel and believe that we were at war with the Middle East, with Islam, and that these were both synonymous with terrorism.

Although this type of talk didn't sit well with me, it wasn't enough of a problem for me to justify making a fuss. I thought to myself: *this is a few bad apples*. I was not aware at the time that these were reprogramming tactics, nor that I was being programmed to make me a mindless and non-questioning soldier. In the Army, soldiers who do not think and do not question are the most useful to accomplish a mission.

By the second week, I was convinced it was a recipe for disaster to send us to Guantanamo Bay. I was questioning (to myself, of course) why the Army—just like the public educational system—didn't invest any resources in giving us cultural or religious training about Islam. We weren't prepared for the 774 prisoners waiting at GTMO who practiced Islam.

I wondered why the military would invest so much time, money and energy convincing us that the prisoners we would be guarding were the 'worst-of-the-worst', that Islam was the enemy and that we would be guarding members of the Taliban, Al-Qaeda and Bin Laden's drivers and cooks. I questioned why they would expend so much effort telling us that these people would kill us given any opportunity. These questions stayed inside my head, behind the wall labeled 'don't question your superiors'. The answers would soon become clear enough, after I had seen first-hand the result of our indoctrination, demonstrated through interactions between hyped-up soldiers and subjected prisoners.

In retrospect, it was a huge waste of time to teach us the protocols regarding meal-time and how to escort prisoners to the bathroom, because a large portion of what I needed to know I had to teach myself after I got there. Since there was no prior education about the Arabic language (let alone about Islam and what it teaches), the point of learning about our routine duties was a dubious one.

In the Army, there is no incentive for prison-guards to know the culture, history or social habits of their prisoners, nor why the prisoners are even being detained. They are to guard them because superiors have ordered it. Soldiers are tools for those above them—tools to achieve a mission. For a soldier/prison guard to ask 'Why not learn about who the prisoners are?' would be futile; that education was not offered and soldiers were highly discouraged from seeking it out.

The distasteful language being thrown around was not only coming from the soldiers themselves but from something prompted by the information fed to us in our training. If it was something assumed and not explicit, it was nonetheless made crystal clear by the trip my company took to the World Trade Center ruins in New York City. My company and I were bused to what is commonly referred to within the borders of the United States as 'Ground Zero'. Wearing our civilian clothes, we stood and read the comments written by prior visitors to the site. The first fifty writings seemed to blend into each other. These words added to the hateful anti-Islamic thoughts that had been drilled into the heads of the company, so when I pointed and laughed at the phrase 'This is the greatest tragedy to happen to all of mankind,' I unwittingly stood out. It marked me in the eyes of my fellow soldiers. They would soon make me pay for displaying my opinion, each and every time I did so.

I believe this culture is a by-product of our American educational system, one that teaches its students to be ignorant to the lessons of history. Perhaps it was also that the propaganda of hatred had fallen on sympathetic minds that were just waiting for something to justify their already bigoted ideas. Having already given many 'pep-talks' clarifying the bearing we all should demonstrate in our up-coming work at GTMO, our senior officers addressed us once again. My allegiance now in question, I was no doubt the intended audience the following (emphatically given) diatribe was meant for:

"Remember, we are at war with Islam, we are at war with the Middle East, the Arab people. These people hate you, they hate everything about you, and they will kill you the first chance they get. These people hate freedom; they beat their women, cut off the hands of thieves and kill you for drinking alcohol. These people blow up themselves and others to spread their religion of hate across the world. Remember: these are not people. These are hate-filled, evil, terrorist dirt-farmers, and they will stop at nothing to kill you. NEVER FORGET THIS! NEVER FORGET 9/11! NEVER FORGET WHY WE ARE FIGHTING!"

Now actively oriented towards our new duty station, we departed for GTMO the next day. Unfortunately for me— and the few others who refused to be blinded by the hate programming—the hateful messages from superiors would not stop. The results of this would be seen and felt in very real ways, acted out in a dark hole in the world called Guantanamo Bay, Cuba.

The Armpit of the World

Cuba is a country described as beautiful (think: lush foliage) and is seen as an ideal vacation destination. Visible from the air, however, is an unsightly bald spot called Guantanamo Bay. Whereas the rest of Cuba is lush and green (with an estimated six thousand different species of flowering plants), the land surrounding Guantanamo Bay is barren and dry. As you leave the area of GTMO, things become beautiful again. It is as though American presence there is a disease; that the land knows it is owned by this disease, so it reflects that.

That such an unattractive blight on the world once garnered interest from the United States of America boggles the mind. That is, only if one considers its physical properties and visual merits. While many Americans probably think that U.S. presence there began in 2006 (after disclosure that it was being used to hold terrorist suspects), the bay has been under our control since June 1898 (during the Spanish-American war). Then, in 1903, President Theodore Roosevelt signed a forced rental agreement for two-thousand gold coins a year, to create a semblance of negotiation between the U.S. and Cuba. In 1934, shortly after overthrowing the government, an agreement approved by Fulgencio Batista (who was in control of the Cuban military at the time) made the rental of Guantanamo Bay one of open-ended duration; to Cuba it now means that the location is occupied territory.

The U.S. has consistently denied requests that it be returned to Cuba; it is fitting that the land is used as a place to hold prisoners, as the land itself is also held captive.

While it may have been established as a naval base or a detention center to hold other peoples and for other reasons, it is clear that its current purpose is to detain suspected terrorists. The day after our visit to the WTC ruins, my company was on our way to GTMO to guard those prisoners and to protect America from them and their ilk.

Having landed in the armpit of Cuba, we boarded a ferry which took us from the airport, across the bay, to buses that were waiting to drive us to Camp Delta (GTMO Bay Detention Facility). *Wait, Cuba is supposed to be tropical; this place looks like a desert*, I thought to myself. As we exited the ferry, my sergeant barked at us to 'Drop your sacks and grab your packs!' and march to the waiting buses. I sat in the second row, at the front of the bus, watching the driver curse while he abruptly zigzagged through the road, dodging iguanas, banana rats, and huge fallen cacti.

"Why not just run over them?" I asked the driver.

"The rats and lizards are endangered—it's against the rules," he replied, his face filled with frustration.

The amount of attention the Army put into protecting the indigenous vermin there was in stark contrast to the extreme lack of care given to the caged human beings who shared that desolate patch of earth. As the camouflage-colored bus rattled on, I saw that this type of wildlife was probably the only kind that could survive there: huge endangered iguanas and banana rats that claw, squirm, and burrow around the black rocks and soil, occasionally setting off the land mines near the base's perimeter. I would spend much time chasing more than one banana rat towards the guard shacks and sally-ports to quell near-riots from prisoners. The prisoners were endlessly scared of these beasts inhabiting GTMO beach; when banana rats snuck into a cell block, just seeing them made the detainees (grown men) scream like children. There are spiders living in the Middle East the size of dinner plates that will chase you while hissing, but these men were used to those creatures. Banana rats can reach the size of large cats; their larger size just means they are that much more detestable.

Intermittent beaches, rocky shores, dying palms and fields of dead grass inhabit Guantanamo Bay, along with the naval base established there. It is the perfect location for a secret military detention facility: no one would guess that anyone would want to work or live there. That any form of life could prosper (or merely survive) on that dying crust of earth is unimaginable.

My first response was wishing I had a dimmer switch for the sun. The brightness of the place was blinding, primarily because of Cuba's proximity to the Equator and (secondarily) because of the lack of trees for shade. My company began another 'hurry-up-and-wait' exercise—through 'in-processing' at the base—as we received our orientation, including where things were, where to shop, what to eat and a review of the many things to do in our spare time. I encountered SFC Neffer again, the funny character who first delivered the news about GTMO. He would sing for us in a loud, annoying voice songs only he remembered the lyrics to, as we traveled by bus to and from work each day.

We were greeted by General Miller, dressed in civilian clothing (from whose command the use of stress positions and music torture were initiated at GTMO). My company and I underwent a brief orientation to SOP that afternoon, were shown a PowerPoint presentation and, after changing into our military uniforms, had a tour of Camp Delta to see the layout of the base. Going through our first tour of GTMO, we were shown the camp setup. The tour of the camps (including construction sites for future camps) went quickly. Then we headed for another part of Delta: the isolation blocks. Over the loudspeaker boomed, "General Miller, General Miller, you're needed at JIF Camp 1. Please pick up the nearest phone, General Miller." Smiling, he wished us luck on our first day of shadowing, dismissed himself, and left a senior MP to finish our orientation to GTMO.

We walked past three different isolation blocks ('Mike', 'November', and 'Oscar') housed in Delta. This short, thirty-something MP took over the tour and began to explain:

"If a detainee refuses to eat, refuses to comply with his shower schedule, is caught defecating anywhere other than his toilet, or is acting out in any way that disturbs the peace and operation of your block, 'isolation' or the threat of it can de-escalate a situation fast, people." We were shown the isolation cells: with only a small slit for fresh air, a toilet, and a small mat to sleep on, they didn't look pleasant. My company followed our guide back to Camp 1 and upon entering we saw a prisoner that I would later come to know as Ruhal: a member of the infamous 'Tipton Trio'. He grabbed the cell bars, kicked the mesh that was attached to them, and yelled at us.

"Welcome home, boys! Do you know where you are?" "Do you know who is sleeping with your girlfriends and sisters at home?" The guard giving the tour slammed his baton against the metal bars and Ruhal backed up, smirking at us, raising his hands and saying, "Just a joke, just a joke for these American boys." I detected a British accent, which surprised me more than what he had said.

There are men here from Western countries? I thought to myself.

We had our morning briefing and were told that we would be shadowing the outgoing unit for the next two weeks, and then would take over for them. This sort of on-the-job training is how the Army works. As we arrived at Camp Delta for our first day of shadowing, we entered the sally-port, which would become an ever-present annoyance. Whereas a gate is simply a gate, a sally-port is comprised of two gates: one for ingress, the other for egress. Army protocol requires that one be searched and inspected while in any sally-port, whereas with an ordinary gate one is not. Sally-ports were control measures to ensure that prisoners did not escape and that nothing was taken into or out of the camp. People were routinely searched, as were vehicles; anything entering or exiting the camp was searched. We were searched entering the camp, leaving the camp, and entering the sections inside each camp. It was a ridiculous security procedure, especially to be held and searched within a camp, all after one had just been searched upon entering the camp itself. Roughly one-hundred and thirty members of my company were searched, and then we assembled in a meeting area just inside the camp for a briefing.

"You will be working inside the camp today: you will be interacting with the 'worst-of-the-worst', with terrorists and Al-Qaeda, with Taliban and extremists alike," we were told. This 'information' was to be repeated far too many times to us during our time at GTMO, as though something might dissuade us of it (common sense?). After our briefing we were grouped with the incoming shift, and then sent on our way to our respective blocks. I was, at this point, expecting to find the 'worst-of-the-worst' waiting for me in those cells. I had had in my head an image of Laurence of Arabia, of men on horseback with gigantic beards and swords. How disappointed I felt when the first thing I heard was a prisoner about six cells down on the left, loudly rapping an Eminem song. When I got down to where he was, I questioned him.

"Why are you rapping? Doesn't Islam hate rap, and all music?" I asked him. The prisoner snapped an answer back.

"No man, Islam does not hate all music, or rap for that matter. I am rapping to keep my spirits high, and my brothers' spirits high," the prisoner answered back in his British accent. This was Ruhal Ahmed, whom I had encountered the previous day. His answer blew me away, and was the first of many epiphanies which would cleanse from my soul any traces of an 'us-versus-them' mentality. I understood at that very moment that my fellow soldiers and I had been lied to, horrifically. I had felt that the warnings about hatred from the prisoners—and how different they were—were dubious, but I hadn't expected the unprofessional behavior I would witness my first day on the job. As I shadowed the guards, I saw protocol breached right and left: prisoners were not always shackled when leaving a cell, and there were not two guards to every prisoner who was out of his cell. These things were just SOP. The guards whom we had come to replace had what is called 'short-timer syndrome', meaning they didn't care about protocol anymore. As a result, my fellow newbies and I were starting out by learning the wrong way to manage daily affairs.

As the outgoing unit was training us—and as my unit took control—the overall feeling in the camp changed. Knowing there was fresh blood on patrol, the prisoners wanted to see how far they could push matters and get away with it. Some in the higher command wanted to see just how far they could push things and still maintain control. In between were the unfortunate soldiers, low in rank such as myself, stuck with training that left much to be desired. This toxic mix of people was a recipe for disaster, one that led to the hell that has been described repeatedly in the media. Few people realize or care what it was like for the soldiers working in that kind of environment, but for me and those like me who wanted simply to work and serve our country in a dignified, regulated, and professional way, it reached a tormenting level.

Being a good soldier was as essential a part of the mission as, say, the cafeteria food. I followed orders and did what I was told, although what I was told to do left a lot to be desired in terms of SOP. Knowing what we were supposed to be doing (and falling short of that because of the issues with our on-the-job training) put us on-edge, like walking on eggshells. Taken together with my individually held beliefs, evidently different from that of others working with me, the result was that I never got comfortable, not in my own skin—not for a minute.

One of the first things to present difficulty for me was the use of certain labels I disliked from the outset.

The term 'general' has a very literal and important meaning to a soldier in the Army, so when I heard the smiling, loud-mouthed prisoner referred to as a 'little general', I wondered: *Was that prisoner given that moniker because he was suspected of having rank in his assumed terrorist organization? If so, why weren't all the ones referred to as 'general' housed in the ISO blocks?* I soon realized that the label 'general' was given to any prisoner familiar with the situation at GTMO: those with advanced communication skills, the ability to get in the faces of their captors, make demands in English, and proclaim their innocence in convincing diatribes. The labeling began with MPs, commenting on the social status of the given prisoner, but it didn't end there; the DOC and all of my superiors used the label to describe prisoners they thought were withholding knowledge, or were recalcitrant—to any degree that justified the use of extreme measures.

I found that although the tag 'general' was assigned by low-ranking soldiers (not the interrogation force), the label created a spiral of mistrust and suspicion. Where someone might enter the camp as a prisoner of little interest, they could be tagged 'little general' by a soldier in sarcastic mockery. That would certainly arouse the interest of the interrogation force which would, for no other reason, interrogate and torture the prisoner incessantly. No inquiry was ever conducted to determine the simple way that these prisoners received this ill-fated nickname. Not one among them, the MPs or the higher-ups, considered that they might themselves behave the same way if imprisoned and interrogated unjustly.

Through the main gate at Camp Delta, Camp 4 lay to the left, with Camps 2 and 3 to the right; directly ahead was Camp 1. At the time I was there, Camps 5 and 6 had not yet been built, but would later be completed in 2006. To gain entrance to each of these camps, we would pass through two sally-ports, the second of them right next to the JIF and DOC locations. The guards closed the first set of sally-ports before the second set opened. Camps 1-4 are all located inside the Delta complex; I worked in Camp 4 during my first three months. General Miller had explained to us upon our arrival that the camps were assigned numbers in the order in which they were completed, so the assigned number did not reflect a security status, in contrast to the scary-looking signs outside each camp. Each camp had the same type of cells, the same blocks—no air-conditioning (AC) for the general population—and large fans set up in the recreation areas. Individual AC units were installed in the ISO blocks but not—it would soon become clear—for comfort. The actual security level of each area could not be ascertained by looking at its physical structure, but rather by the condition of its prisoners—which required closer investigation.

Camp Delta was comprised of six-hundred and twelve units that housed the general population at GTMO. There were three ISO blocks. The cells housed between twenty-four and forty-eight prisoners to a block; each cell had prison bars with interlaced metal-mesh. Each block had an office where the block sergeant would be on duty, while a few guards walked up and down the block. Prisoners made a game of communicating with each other from across the hallways, which were about four or five meters wide.

The cells in Camp Echo were larger than in Delta; the prisoners held there were thought by the interrogators to have high-value information—'prosecutable' cases. Camp Echo is approximately a quarter mile away from Camps 1-4. Ironically, Ahmed Errachidi (Detainee 590) (who maintained his innocence and was finally set free without charge), and David Hicks, who admittedly fought alongside anti-coalition forces, were held there exclusively for quite some time. Guards working in Camp Echo worked longer shifts, and guarded only one or two prisoners at a time, as opposed to the 24 to 48 hour shifts my team and I worked at Camp Delta.

The population fluctuated a good deal in Camp Echo with the interrogation force's changing opinion on who was most interesting at the moment. It housed a low number of high-value prisoners in larger ISO units.

Camp Iguana is about a mile away from Camp Delta. I didn't see it right away. The young 'terrorists'—two 12-year-olds and one 13-year-old—were kept there. I was told they received proper treatment, as proper as prisoner children thousands of miles away from their families could receive. Their privileges included TV hours and swimming in the ocean. I was told they were counseled emotionally and mentally, and received an education in their native language while there, as well as English as a second language.

Then there was 'Camp No'. It was nicknamed that, but was actually Camp 7, also called "The General's Cottage". While I never saw this camp myself—only heard rumors of it—I nonetheless understood that any high-value prisoner brought there would later be permanently segregated from the rest of the population, as it was that secret. There was also another camp that was being worked by an entirely different and separate branch of the government to which my fellow soldiers and I were never privy.

There were many surprises and secrets to be revealed as I worked and learned in GTMO in the coming year. These surprises were not pleasant, and broke something inside my heart.

Camp Delta was where I shadowed, and would end up working the majority of my time in GTMO. It was a mercy that I was assigned to Camp 4 at first; prisoners in that camp were on the whole more agreeable and, as I would discover, more talkative. They were given more comfort items such as board games and toilet paper, and didn't have to wear orange jumpsuits. Ruhal Ahmed said in an interview later that Camp Delta was where those that had gone crazy from the torture were housed. They were broken, and so had fewer inhibitions about conversing with the guards. They would talk with the guards, and were very polite and hospitable, so guards didn't need to use shackles at all times. There were group cells and bunks, and also areas called recreation rooms in which ten prisoners could socialize and dine. Tables were found inside, and eventually even some exercise equipment.

The heat was the enemy of both the guards and prisoners: prisoners would perpetually argue over who would have to sit closest to the fan because it became difficult to sleep directly in front of it. The guards were in a regular habit of removing and replacing them for the prisoners, as the heat was constant and intense.

The AC units, as mentioned, were installed in the ISO cells, but were more for delivering extreme cold (as a punishment) than for comfort, or to give the illusion of mercy during more civilized interrogations.

Ruhal Ahmed has said that the interrogation rooms were small, approximately three by four meters, with a table at the center. Sometimes the chair had a cushion, and other times just the plastic seat. Linoleum lined the floors, and a two-way mirror was installed on one side. On the floor was a large hook to which the prisoners were shackled if physical abuse was in order.

As a gesture of good treatment, Halaal meals were delivered two times daily (medical and dental care were provided as well), but I discovered that this did not mean that prisoners were treated humanely. It was a wonder to me that taxpayers' money was funneled into the place. When I first arrived, I had hoped that it was for some greater purpose that would produce some beneficial return on that investment. In time, I recognized that any benefit to the U.S. was nil, and so I decided to seek out benefit for myself.

That first night I slept in temporary housing, which was only one hundred yards from Camp Delta. From my room, I heard the adhan, the Islamic call to prayer. Many people, upon hearing the call to prayer live, or from a proper recording, say that it is beautiful and melodious and even welcoming. However, as Islam was ugly to those who presided over GTMO, the adhan was intentionally exaggerated and stretched out of proportion until it was mutilated beyond recognition. While it was played on the loudspeakers five times a day at the correct prayer times, the recording was distorted beyond belief by the sound system. The sound coming out of the speakers sounded more like a screech, indiscernible and very hard on the ears. Just as with the Halaal meats, the U.S. Army wanted to portray an outward display of consideration for Islam, but in fact just wanted to make a mockery of it. The effect of the distortion of the adhan was not lost on the soldiers who might have been soothed by the beautiful words and meaning of the call to prayer:

Allahu Akbar, Allahu Akbar

Allahu Akbar, Allahu Akbar

(God is the Greatest)

Ash-hadu an laaaa ilaaahaa il Allaaah

Ash-hadu an laaaa ilaaahaa il Allaaah

(I bear witness that there is no deity but Allah)

Ash-hadu anna Muhammad ar Rasool Allah

Ash-hadu anna Muhammad ar Rasool Allah

(I bear witness that Muhammad is the Messenger of Allah)

Hay,ya Alaas-Salaaah, Hay,ya Alaas-Salaaah

(Come to the prayer)

Hay,ya Alaal FaalaaaH, Hay,ya Alaal FaalaaaH

(Come to success)

Allahu Akbar, Allahu Akbar

Laaaa ilaaahaa il Allaaah

(There is no deity except Allah)

Soldiers new to the base covered their ears when it would play, but they eventually got used to it, and found it as abrasive and caustic as the sweltering heat.

After three weeks there (in Army-speak: soon), we then moved into what would be our residence while at GTMO. The two-story condos constituted a small complex of what looked like very small houses. They were the type of stucco houses you'd see on any suburban street in America; perhaps they were meant to give that illusion for those missing home. Each typically housed six to eight soldiers, sharing two bathrooms, a kitchen, a living room, two bedrooms and a master bedroom. It was only in the house that I felt comfortable sorting out my thoughts about what occurred each day. The contrast between the superficial training we had received stateside and the harsh realities at GTMO loomed in my awareness. Leaving my townhouse to enter this seething cauldron of fear and hatred, I was confronted with a raging war. Although the outcome of the conflict was unclear, the combatants were realigning within me, flanking my soul.

They say that in the Army, the men are mighty fine...

Tossing and turning through that first night at GTMO, I kept hearing the mysterious Arabic 'chant' in my ears. Blasted through the speakers, distorted and annoying to others, it touched a place inside my soul, a place that called to me. I would answer that call soon enough. That morning, I awoke from a restless sleep, showered, put on my BDU and headed to the chow hall to see what Uncle Sam was cooking for breakfast.

After a few days of shadowing the other MPs I had learned all of their responsibilities: escorting prisoners to and from wherever they needed to go during the day, serving Halaal meals in their little picnic area, searching cells for contraband or forbidden comfort items, supplying prisoners with replacement clothing when needed, and ensuring that prisoners were not corresponding with each other via notes. The prisoners in my blocks were quite masterful at communicating with one another, using threads from their clothes; they would pass notes through the use of thread-made slings.

I was officially assigned to Camp 4, the minimum-security area where I quickly came to a much clearer understanding about the reality of where I was. Our own trainers—the senior guards at GTMO—now supervised us, overseeing the new guards who would be writing in the log-book. Within just a few days, the decision was made to return the older company training us to a passive state; the trainers took the back seat to let us assume control. Their indolence and inflexibility made the transition difficult. There were countless times that the prisoners themselves had to tell me or my fellow soldiers that we were doing something in an incorrect manner.

"MP, MP, that is not how you do that, you need to open the bean-hole first," the prisoners explained. They also made other suggestions. Being self-assured as newbies tend to be, we would often reply, arrogantly.

"Excuse me detainee; I'm pretty sure I know what I am doing," while in the back of our minds we wondered if the prisoners were indeed correct. Those who cared to find out could go and look in the SOP manual and see that the prisoners were (usually) correct. This was their turf—their home—and they knew better than the new blood on the cellblock. However, it only proved to me again that these prisoners were not as we had been told. If these men were indeed the 'worst-of-the-worst', they would have tried to exploit the new guards' lack of knowledge to cause trouble and mayhem. Oddly, the prisoners were instead making sure that things were done correctly, to prevent any incidents that might occur. They were, incredibly, assisting the guards in doing a better job, overall.

I considered these 'towel-heads' and 'dirt farmers'. They were polite. They were educated—often multilingual—college or university graduates. They were willing to teach those over them their shortcomings with the aim of maintaining order...and peace.

I learned quickly that the prisoners were willing both to help me do my job and to treat me respectfully as long as I respected them, so I tried my utmost to uphold the golden rule. Instead of walking on the block each morning with a 'damn filthy animals, let's kill them all!' attitude like some of my comrades, I asked how I could build a bridge, each day, to cross that wide gap between guard and prisoner, between East and West. Unorthodox and optimistic, it resulted in both joy and pain, and produced an air of relief. It was a difficult enough job, and since hatred is more emotionally draining than compassion, my intention at first was just to make life there a little easier for myself by making it easier for them. While some of those my unit and I were replacing seemed to have a respectful, working relationship with the prisoners, those in my unit were taking a different approach. *What harm could it do*, I thought to myself, *to come to work with a positive attitude and try to be pleasant throughout the day while interacting with prisoners?*

My first memories of GTMO are the mealtimes and taking the prisoners to and from interrogations. I would talk with my friend Peck (another MP) about things that were occurring around the base and try to pretend, for a moment, that what we were doing wasn't a disastrous mistake—one of colossal proportions—that it would not leave permanent scars. Peck was assigned work at Camp Echo, so I didn't see him very often after those early days. We both had the chance to meet the more notorious prisoners: the General, Lefty, David Hicks, and the Tipton Trio. Peck's experience, together with that of others', would help us reframe and resolve our experiences after work.

One might imagine that at an American military base would start each day with the "The Star-Spangled Banner" (the national anthem of the U.S.A). That was my assumption, at least. However, at GTMO the COC propounded a consistent message: revenge. That is the message that the video—played inside the chow hall every morning—continuously relayed. On my first day at work, I smelled the tasty food and filled a plate for breakfast. A familiar song boomed throughout the chow hall from a sound system connected to two televisions at the back of the room: the hard-hitting, pivotal part of the soundtrack from the film *Terminator 2: Judgment Day*. The hairs on the back of my neck stood up, my pulse racing. I felt a rush of adrenaline as though I were in the middle of watching some epic movie preview. Soldiers looked around, smiling at each other as a blood-lusting yell blasted through the speakers in the ceiling corners of the room. It was the beginning of the heavy metal Drowning Pool song "Bodies Hit the Floor". Played loudly, it accompanied a military video of F-14 fly-bys, explosions, images of captives with bags over their heads, and aircraft carriers full of planes flaunting their power. In the video, American flags were flapping in the wind.

An intermittent, scrolling message rolled down like drops of blood in front of the 'promotional' video, addressed to the Taliban in Afghanistan, reading: "The U.S. Forces will seek you out and kill you, if you don't surrender. We will kill you, bomb you, and find you wherever you are." Although my appetite was kindled choosing my breakfast, I now felt nauseous. My excitement deflated almost immediately and I stopped mid-bite. Peach cobbler and waffles sat untouched as I watched my fellow MPs jumping onto tables, victoriously holding their chairs above their heads, and head-banging to "Bodies Hit the Floor". A plastic smile screwed on my face, now unable to eat, I stood

45

up and threw my entire breakfast into the trash. This same video was unfortunately played each morning, replacing the national anthem, a message neither to the Taliban nor our prisoners, but to us soldiers, that we were no longer in America with its structure and regulations: that none of those rules applied here. Each day (and at other military functions) this video fed the already vengeful attitude of the soldiers at GTMO. My soul felt as empty as my stomach that first day as I started work at GTMO. Where other soldiers were energized for their day, my morale was drained as I left the chow hall in a state reserved only for those surrounded with adversity.

So many revelations occurred, revelations that would undermine the noble reasons I had for joining the military. One such revelation was the secret existence of other prison camps run by the U.S. at Guantanamo Bay. I had seen other camps on arrival, near the airstrip, and one day I inquired about them.

"We don't work at those camps, they are for the Haitians," replied a trainer. *What do you mean, we don't work them?* I thought to myself. A list of questions formed in my mind: *Who does? Were there other people on the island working in another prison system? Were they capturing those trying to escape their country to come to America?* The idea that the base at GTMO would share the small peninsula with groups we were not made aware of, or worked alongside with, irked me. Further information about that area was evidently classified (secret), so too was information regarding the other camps in GTMO (beyond those I worked); neither of which I was allowed to investigate. I also saw a disconnection between the various branches of the U.S. Military, divided and insulated from one another—which was, to say the least, very iNeffericient. It did not lend itself well to a feeling of confidence or security.

The new unit was soon working at full speed. All members of my unit were assigned to our stations. My station, Camp 4, was where prisoners were kept who were either compliant with the interrogation groups, or were going home soon. While other guards assigned to higher-security areas were intentionally disrespecting prisoners, I enjoyed a more complacent and relaxed work atmosphere. I didn't witness that kind of hell until later. Working with ten prisoners to one guard,

I worked in a camp that had a communal living situation where the prisoners served themselves. I interacted with them on a daily basis. My time in Camp 4 was to my liking, primarily because it afforded me all the time in the world to build those aforementioned bridges, talking with the prisoners. In 12-hour shifts, those working Camp 4 and I did PT on our own and ate on our own; we were a unit within the unit. The men we were guarding were from over forty-five different countries, some of which I had never heard of. I was excited at the opportunity to speak to people from all over the world about where they came from—to enrich my worldly knowledge. A firm believer in little else than 'everything happens for a reason', I wanted the chance to positively transform the disheartening experience I'd had since landing in Cuba.

The other two MPs on the block in Camp Delta and I began by spending most of our time walking up and down the block. I counted the cell bars, the little windows, noting the many small arrows pointing east that had been drawn with spray paint. I counted the steps from one side of the block to the other to pass the time. My one-minute 'vacations' (smoke breaks) couldn't come soon enough. It was terribly monotonous; and also awkward, and not being able to speak Arabic was the most obvious challenge.

When it was time to serve food, I would escort the prisoners to a small picnic area adjacent to their room. This was a daily routine, unless I was working the night shift. I would oversee two rooms of ten men who were eating: I would walk into the small picnic area with a cart full of food—literally just twenty non-shackled prisoners and me. That I had no other soldiers, nor baton, nor other weapon for protection, and that no other guard could see me (except one in a tower at the far end of the camp) disturbed me, at first. However, there was never any incident. In fact, as was demonstrated in their helpfulness during the training period, the prisoners would help me perform my duties. They would help me get the food off the cart, and then serve each other. When finished, they would even help me clean up and reload the cart after eating. Although prisoners caused certain disruptions at GTMO and guards exercised discipline tactics, to both guards and prisoners, food was inviolable. Those on the hunger strikes—a horrifying experience I later witnessed—were the only exception.

Other duties included escorting prisoners to recreation, shower, and interrogation. Through all of it, I kept to myself. I busied myself observing the prisoners' behavior, and listening to the lingo and buzzwords around camp: 'general', 'ERF', and a thousand Arabic words I quickly learned. I watched other MPs to see just how seriously they took their jobs, as I had already noticed failures in the COC (discipline, etc.). After almost a month, everyone started bending little rules here and there, myself included. Why adhere to protocol and stand out? My mindset already separated me from the pack.

As I walked the halls to pass time, the somber realities of the place sunk in deeper and deeper. It numbed me to myself, to my fellow man, and to God; what little relationship I had with any of them. It wasn't easy to distance myself: everyone eyeballed me, I eyeballed them back, and when I walked by, they would all say things in Arabic or other languages that were foreign to me. I didn't like being ignorant of what they were saying, even if it was negative. The language issue was at least one area where I could try to be understood.

When I came out of my shell from time to time, I met characters working with me that would become important as I spent my long year at GTMO. Private Michael, a good guy to bum a smoke from, was the cool, quiet black guy I recalled from training. Then there was the corn-fed, older, white boy named Smitty. Smitty had obviously been at GTMO much longer than I had. He would often stand around talking with whatever sergeant was on duty when we weren't busy and gravitated to the end of the block furthest from me. Right away I didn't like him—he wasn't cool.

I struggled to fit in and find friends. Other than Peck, Pvt. Michael, Bradley and Pvt. Enrique, my roommate, I could recognize faces but had no names. Hundreds of interactions each day passed by without exchange of names. There were two reasons for this: first, it was covered on their BDU, and second, they didn't care to talk with me outside the detention facility. The COC's idea of recreation was water-sports and softball, both of which I loathed. So I used my free time getting better at chess strategies, writing letters to my wife, trading stories with my few friends, smoking, and practicing Arabic with home-made flashcards. I also chatted online with other people who spoke Arabic to get a better handle on the language and its usage, which I didn't consider harmful in the least. Good ol' boy Smitty did, however, and informed SSG Johnsville and Sgt. Parks. Almost instantly, they attempted to intimidate me with idle threats of being locked up in GTMO myself if I did not cease my outside education.

Bradley and I became buddies. We hung out when time permitted, scheduled to smoke and eat around the same times, and when we were off, otherwise hung out together. I found a sympathetic ear in Bradley as I expressed myself about how wrong things were at GTMO.

Each time I witnessed despicable conduct, I bumped up my bridge-building by getting some Arabic tips from the prisoners, and conversed with them at length. Indeed, I found that the prisoners were great conversationalists, had interesting things to say, and that the talks I would have, however short, would yield a wealth of information about the world.

It afforded me an escape, at least in my mind. This different approach to guarding the prisoners went against the dominant paradigm: that one should just do his job without question. One should never question oneself or anyone else about, for example, roughing up a prisoner during routine cell switches. The regular code of conduct was that if the rules were broken, guards would not talk about it. Afterwards, they would return to their company, blend in as best they could, and take part in the provided recreation. If they didn't conform to that routine, they were singled out.

One could not say that in those first six months I did not make an honest effort to get with the program. I was merely trying to find a comfortable place, on a sweltering hot, black rock in the desert, without getting burned.

Enemy Mine

One day, while walking along the cellblocks, I heard more than just the usual whispers. This time I heard a prisoner singing, and the sound got louder with each step I took as I headed towards the end of the block. The other prisoners nearby were watching the singer. I smiled as I recognized the hit Eminem song by the lyrics: *Slim Shady, brain dead like Jim Bradley, I'm a M80, you Lil' like that Kim lady...* The entertaining prisoner had his back turned to me and threw his arms into the air as he sung louder to his cellmates, *So when you see me on that block with my glocks screaming, F*** the world like Tupac, I just don't give a f****. He smiled—a few prisoners even clapped—and he turned around, smiling at me. I saw that it was the same prisoner who had yelled at us on our way through our initial tour of Camp 4.

"Oh, it's you, the Little General, huh?" I remarked, hoping for a clue as to how the prisoners liked being referred to by that nickname.

The prisoner looked at me and hissed, with a proud smile on his face.

"I'm not the General, American boy," the prisoner snapped back. "I'm Ruhal. These are my brothers, and we are the famous GTMO band called the 'GTMO Caribbean Trio'. You like our outfits?" It was the first time I had heard a prisoner refer to GTMO by name, and the first time I had heard sarcasm in reference to it. I kept my silence, as a respectful member of any audience will do when he senses the performance isn't over. Ruhal then addressed all who could hear him. "Hello, hello American boy, Christian boy, do you like Eminem? I'll sing Eminem, Snoop Dogg for you, and you bring me a Coca-Cola. I'll trade you for your American fruit-juice and water, just one can of Coke, huh American boy? Can you hear me? Which song should I sing now?"

Both sides of the block had stopped whatever they were doing and began listening to Ruhal. A few prisoners were now laughing and shouting at each other across the hall in Arabic words I couldn't yet understand. I turned and looked at

51

Ruhal, with his proud, devout comrades behind him, thumbing prayer beads or exercising, trying not to laugh at his antics. They were waiting for my reaction to his singing and comments.

"So, do all good Muslims usually sing American music, and Eminem?" I asked, answering the question with a question. Ruhal looked at me and then turned his head to his two brothers lying in their bunks. They nodded and smiled knowingly.

"I don't claim to be a good Muslim. I am always trying to be a better Muslim, though." The reply hit me like a brick. The noise on the block from the other prisoners died down, and I faced the long corridor, thinking to myself: *How can you be a better Muslim in prison?* Then, a question more profound in my awareness surfaced: *How can you be a good person inside a prison?* I felt like a good person. I had joined the military to demonstrate my desire to be a better American. I felt it was obvious that GTMO was an awkward place for personal improvement of any sort. Looking at two other MPs, I noticed the MP furthest down the hall staring at me. Then he said something into his two-way radio.

"Everything okay down there, Private?"

I hit the two-way on my shoulder and quickly responded to quell any anxiety from the other guards, "Everything's okay. I settled some loud correspondence over here and everyone's relaxing now."

"Okay."

I felt that an opening had been created, and I wanted to see to what extent I could gain deeper insight or knowledge from these men. I wanted to see how long I could keep the conversation going around self-improvement, and Islam.

"None of your friends behind you understand a word when you sing, do they?"

Ruhal smirked at me and said, "Not really. Not unless I am singing in Arabic, no."

"Then why do it?"

"In Islam, almost all music is forbidden. In Britain, where my brothers and I are from, music is always playing in the stores, the public transit, and public places of all kinds. This is very melodic to you, though, yes?" Ruhal began.

"I suppose some music is, but they don't play rap music in shopping malls or grocery stores buddy...well, not the good stuff anyway," I replied.

"Unless it is the word of Allah, or someone singing their praises to Allah, it offends the ears of true believers. Besides, this is already a place that disrespects Islam, and is a black-eye to America. So why not sing Eminem? Why not sing something about how you as a society hate yourselves?" In surprised silence, I listened intently as Ruhal continued, "If you were shopping with your children, gone to market to buy dinner, or at your church praying, would you feel comfortable surrounded by strangers with Eminem's music playing loudly? You might like the music, but its meaning is lost on the people who don't understand its passion. They just hear a disruption, so a disruption it becomes, yes?"

I laughed a little to myself thinking about the Drowning Pool military video that I had trained myself to block out so I could eat breakfast each morning. "You know Ruhal: I think I might know something about disruptive music." Ruhal smiled, sensing we had found some rare middle ground. I smiled too, and jokingly questioned Ruhal. "Who are the other members of your band? They don't look like they sing."

"These are my brothers, Shafiq and Asif. They are devout Muslims, better than I: their prayers provide solace during my stay here." He picked up his Quran and finished speaking, "The Words of Allah have the same meaning here as they would anywhere else."

I stepped closer to the cell, nearly out of view to the MP nearest the officer's booth. I whispered to Ruhal now, while slowly stepping towards the right end of the cell, a question not for retort but for information, "You think it is possible to be a good Muslim in prison, then?" Ruhal followed me to that side and whispered back.

"It's possible to be that and much more. Ask the one everyone's been calling the 'Professor': he can tell you about Muslim people in Britain, and about being a good Muslim, and about why we should be in our beds with our wives, not here." Recognizing the name 'Professor', I nodded to Ruhal and turned around to start patrolling the block with the other two MPs again. Everything took on a different hue after that exchange. As I patrolled the block that day, I thought of the old movies where prisoners would bang their cups on the bars, or reach out to their jailers to grab their keys and annoy their captors. What a splendid, kind way to stick it to the man, I thought: sing him the songs of his home country.

What I, and especially the more aggressive and bigoted guards, wouldn't know is that when we made mockery of Islam, it made prisoners like Ruhal—Muslims largely in name only—only more firm in their faith, in their practice. Indeed, it was due to the adversity caused by the persistent insults towards Muslims and Islam that the prisoners were strengthened, renewing their practice even more intensely. For example, Ruhal Ahmed and learned Arabic and learned to read the Quran while imprisoned at GTMO. The guards would tell the inmates, 'Shave your beard and we'll let you go home', and 'Stop praying. Stop practicing your religion, and we'll let you out of here'. A thinking prisoner would reason that the war being waged had little to do with their nationality or where they were seized by coalition forces. Rather, it was their identification as Muslims—this made them strong.

The floodgates were now open in my mind. When among some of the prisoners who had noted my interest in Islam and the Quran, I spent much of any time I had asking questions.

"Why do you pray in that funny language?"

"Why do you pray facing the East?"

"What is the Ka'aba?"

"Who is Allah? Who is Muhammad?"

"How do you feel about Christians?"

"What do you think of Jews?"

And, although not intending to provoke, "Why do you think 9/11 happened?"

As annoying as these questions might have been to the prisoners, they tried their best to answer them. When asked by my superiors why I spent so much time talking to the prisoners, I would reply with a smart answer such as: "Sun Tzu said 'Know thy enemy', so I am just learning more about my enemy."

Camp 4 was an ideal place for me to learn and maintain contact with individuals who didn't mind answering my growing list of questions. Soldiers working in that camp worked alone more often than not, and contact with supervisors was minimal. In this way, I began to learn the fundamentals of Islam. No matter how simple or bothersome the questions were, the prisoners always treated me with respect. My questions were answered humbly, without telling me that I had to become a Muslim myself to discover the answers I sought. They did not present Islam as the only way, or even the right way, but simply their way, answering my questions with gentle grace. One prisoner took such an interest in me and my thirst for knowledge that he gave me his Quran and his prayer mat.

My mind was already made up that the Quran would be a book of nonsense, like other religious texts I had read. Through my reading of folklore, magic stories, poems, hymns and theological essays, I had collected in my mind small nuggets of truth to sustain my life. How surprised I was when I opened the Quran and began to read the words of God Himself. Aside from the task of reading *Surah al Baqarah,* with its historical details of the tribes of Israel and the tribulations the Jewish people faced in ancient times, the rest of the Quran I found to be a simple instruction manual for living. No hypocrisy, belief in magic or unseen forces was required. I had already read the Old and New Testaments a few times, to see what my grandmother liked about them so much. I had perused the Bhagavad Gita, the Torah, some of the Nordic traditions, literature from Paganism, Satanism and Wicca in order to argue better with those I saw as foolish. Reading the Quran was like seeing a huge light-bulb of logic, illuminating the dark world of ideas that had previously clouded my mind.

I had viewed blind subservience to organized religion as a simplistic, hypocritical, dualistic and conflicted way to live. People would justify their wrongdoing, such as murder, in the name of God. I had seen people touting 'The Lord's Work', and seen those same people go against every teaching. I had read the books of other religions in order to enlighten others about how misguided they were. But when I read the Quran, I found truth and could find no way to create an argument against its simple, pure pages.

As for those prisoners in Camp 4 who read the Quran as a matter of faith, I could see they were happy and smiling; making good use of the time they had to spend in GTMO. They would wake up and smile, stick to their faith, support each other, and work as a community. This made me wonder two things: first, what was it about Islam that helped them live that way, and second, what would be the daily attitude of seven-hundred and seventy-eight Christian Americans captured and detained somewhere in a miserable hole such as this, in the Middle East?

One would no doubt hear such things as: 'You can't do this to me, I'm an American!', 'You will pay for this!', and 'My country will come save me, and you will pay!' Then, after their initial aggression, there would be mournful pleas such as: 'Why God, why me?', 'Why would God do this to me?' before, eventually, 'There can't be a God at all, or else I wouldn't have been put here.'

I would hear the prisoners call out from time to time that they had families and they were innocent, that we had no business locking them up like animals. However, those saying these things would not allow misery to swallow them, and instead they would carry on smiling, joking, learning, reading and interacting with others, prisoners and guards alike. I had several questions that I posed to them.

"How can you be so happy when you do not know why you are here?"

"How can you smile not knowing how your family is doing without you?"

"How can you live day-to-day not knowing when you will be set free from this place?"

A single answer came back with clarity and conviction, from prisoner after prisoner:

"This is nothing more than a test of my faith. This is a test in life. The next life is what matters. Allah is testing my faith."

Whether or not they were on the right path, or whether any religion was right for me, I was impressed that their adherence to their religious beliefs gave them such peace in their minds and hearts. The peaceful attitudes of those prisoners and the Quran's simple guide for living together soothed my soul. They slowly and consistently worked away at me like the waves lapping the sand on the shores of Guantanamo Bay.

Worst of the Worst

I was not to work in Camp 4 my entire time at GTMO. I was sent to work in Camps 1, 2, and 3, which were an entirely different story. These were the maximum-security camps inside Camp Delta. The dispositions of both guards and prisoners were different here: Guards were on high alert and ERFs were deployed frequently, in which four or five men in riot gear with shields would run into the cell of a helpless man who was gasping and had been blinded by OC spray, the guards finding it necessary to throw in some punches or kicks from behind their armor. Tension was high as prisoners were often taken to interrogation there. I thought the guards I worked with in Camp 4 had bad attitudes, but what I experienced of hate and aggression in Camps 1, 2 and 3 made working in Camp 4 seem like a tiptoe through the tulips. In this area of GTMO, the senior guards were worse, working but few hours a day, a few days a week, expressing care for nothing.

Individually caged, the prisoners were less easy-going and harder to talk to, but despite this, I made associates quickly. To those who spoke English, I posed the same questions I had posed before and received similar answers. I asked them personal questions about their worldviews and about Islam. Constantly walking up and down the blocks to prevent unauthorized correspondence between prisoners, I worked with two other MPs I didn't know by name, and SSG Johnsville who was our block sergeant. Other ways these camps differed from Camp 4 were that all of the prisoners were dressed in orange, we only issued toilet paper as needed, and privileges and comfort items had to be earned.

I saw Ahmed Errachidi infrequently in these camps. I remember thinking it was because Errachidi was on the 'frequent flier program', a style of torture which included much interrupted sleep and constant movement from one camp to another. He had been moved between Camp Echo and Camp Delta regularly and had been subjected to a variety of other tortures.

There was a great deal more work the guards were responsible for in these camps, depending on what shifts they were working. The day shift had to serve breakfast, start recreation and shower time, exchange laundry, and complete cell inspections. This continued with swing shift, which had to serve dinner, finish showers and recreation, exchange laundry, and tie up whatever loose ends were left by the day shift. Both shifts were interrupted constantly by interrogations, medics, and prisoner cell movement. Constant supervision of any block was a challenge given routine head counts, minor block issues (and riots), and the resulting prisoner reports of conduct. The night shift had only to clean the block and kill the clock. Since I was low in rank, I usually got the job of cleaning the block, often alone. While there was much to do during the day and swing shifts, and too much supervision to conduct useful conversations with prisoners, the night shift afforded excellent, extended opportunities for me to continue my education. Prisoners who couldn't sleep indulged my questions with a steady flow of answers. Other guards would wonder during the daytime why I was not displaying anger or aggression towards the prisoners. My reply to that was simply that I had started at Camp 4, where I had a relaxed environment and mutual respect. The deeper, concealed answer was that I knew in my heart these men did not deserve to be here, or deserve to have anger and aggression thrown at them from every side. I knew that they were there for a higher reason, and that I was, too. Through my conversations with them, I began to identify more with them than with my fellow soldiers.

I grew tired of seeing Smitty, Parks, and Johnsville berate and trip the prisoners or drag them across the block in shackles, or cut their shower and recreation times short. Johnsville always seemed to be instigating violent behavior towards the prisoners or was himself in the thick of it. Opening the door and getting physical didn't happen as often as I was sure Johnsville would have liked, but every time it did, I knew something was wrong. *This is not the way America operates!* I thought to myself, powerless to do anything to stop it, hating it in my heart. I hoped I could hold out—hating the aggressive behavior and sidestepping any personal involvement—until my release from the hellhole. Author Terry Prachett once wrote,

"Light thinks it travels faster than anything but it is wrong. No matter how fast light travels, it finds the darkness has always gotten there first, and is waiting for it."

One day, unfortunately, I was inevitably dragged into an ERF.

At the beginnings of our shifts, we would have our briefings and be told where we were working and what we needed to know about the coming day. The block sergeant leaving the block would also brief us as we came on. They would mention who was on the ERF that day. Some days I would be selected to be on the ERF, and others I was not. I never bothered to pay attention to what that meant and never cared to ask because the other days I was working, nothing ever came of it.

One morning, we were working the day shift and a prisoner had just returned from an interrogation, one that had evidently gone very badly. Upon return to his cell he told the other prisoners what had happened and all the prisoners around him decided it was time to riot! The call came over the radio:

"ERF team assemble, Tango Block." I paid no attention to it, as I had no idea what an ERF was. Brief training had been provided when I first arrived, but since I hadn't used that knowledge in the first months, I'd forgotten all about it.

"Holdbrooks! Get your a** off this block and get over to Tango Block! There is an ERF!" my block sergeant yelled at me. I didn't know what to do, so I ran out of the block into the sally-port. A group of people were putting on riot gear...and then I remembered what an ERF was. I tried to put on my gear quickly and prepare as I was already late. My superiors were angry with me due to my lateness.

We assembled on the block outside the prisoner's cell. The prisoner had a towel wrapped around his face, took an aggressive stance towards us, and along with the prisoners in the cells around him, was yelling with a great deal of anger. It was pandemonium—so much happening at once. There was no time to think before acting. I looked over to the block sergeant and saw he was standing by and ready, along with all the guards who were working Tango Block. The camp officer was talking to the prisoner, who was angry and aggressive. The prisoner was yelling about wrongdoings—what had been done to him in interrogation—and that he wasn't going to take it any longer. What had happened during the interrogation had incited a riot on the block, and it became clear that he was not going to calm down. The camp officer explained to him that if he did not calm down, he would be sprayed with OC spray.

The prisoner did not calm down.

Procedure dictates the method by which guards are to administer the spray, which is in a swift 'z' motion across the face, just enough to debilitate the prisoner and render him docile. The camp officer went above and beyond as he proceeded to empty nearly half the can of OC spray on the prisoner's face, his clothes, his Quran, and his cell. Waiting the 30 seconds to allow the spray to take effect, the door swung open and the five of us in riot gear flooded into the cell in an effort to further subdue the prisoner. We hog-tied him with plastic zip-ties. In this position it was simple work for the other soldiers to twist his arms so far they might have dislocated them, put his face in the toilet, step on his hands and feet, and upon exiting the cell with him, use his head to open the door. This was accompanied by perfectly placed knees to his kidney. As if all of that weren't enough, jabs and punches to his abdomen completed the assault.

"There is one for America!" the soldiers would exclaim as they dealt their blows. I was a reluctant participant and wondered at their words. *Didn't all the hijackers die on 9/11?*, I thought to myself. *There's one for whom?*

The purpose of the ERF was to de-escalate a situation where a prisoner became aggressive. However, the protocol was breached in several different areas, such as when they extracted the prisoner from his cell. They cleaned him and provided medical aid, but then shaved his beard and his head. Later it was explained to me that they shaved the beard and head because it was easier than the suggested washing and (of course), for a Muslim man, humiliating; it broke down his self-esteem.

SSG Johnsville, upon hearing of my participation, patted me on the back and said, "You did good back there Holdbrooks. I had my doubts about you, but you done good." The sergeant was commenting on a second-hand report, but could well have viewed the video of the ERF, had he so chosen. The military protocol in GTMO was to take video footage of each ERF, in case we got sued or questions arose regarding unfair practices. It was largely for appearances, as the soldier in charge of filming would typically forget to remove the lens cap, charge the camera battery, press record, or place a tape into the camera. I was shocked at my own adrenaline rush—at my participation in such an act—and at the other guards' enthusiasm over their abuse of the prisoner. In my heart I experienced the strange and nauseating mixture of excitement and regret.

The other soldiers, however, clearly got a charge out of the aggression and the physical aspect of ERFs, but it was this experience that convinced me to be a conscientious objector. I thought of my wife and my future and existing family, and of how proud they were of me, and of my eventual career in the Army. I didn't want to lose my career, my wife or my family's respect over this...there had to be another, better, way.

I was rewarded for being one of the 'good ol' boys.' It was not money, medals, or promotion that would demonstrate recognition from the higher-ups. Rather, I was rewarded for fraternization, which is against the rules in the Army. However, I recognized that GTMO (since it was not on U.S. soil) was not subject to conventional rules, morality or Army protocols. It was one of only a few times that I would drink with my superiors. It was then that I began discerning deeper problems. For instance, fraternization—normally forbidden—was co-occurring with rewards for those who displayed a characteristic pattern of verbal and physical aggression. Such soldiers were getting more days off, easier jobs at GTMO, and preferential treatment.

This was when the more extreme members of the aggressive group, dubbed 'the Regime' by soldiers not among them, began making some of their views clear to me:

"Holdbrooks, I was worried about you. I thought you were a sympathizer and that you were going to want to become a

Taliban like all those towel heads in the camp. Holdbrooks, I am glad to see that you were able to do your job and not hesitate. Now I feel sure that you are on our side."

"Holdbrooks, you know we were going to put you in an orange jumpsuit and leave you there at the end of the day with all your sand nigger buddies so you could rot here just like them, but I guess I was wrong, you're a good ol' American after all."

My superiors, who made up what we called 'The Regime', shared these drunken sentiments with me. They may have been veiled threats, or just admissions made through the stupor of alcohol, but they made me very uncomfortable. With all the rule-breaking and breaches of protocol at GTMO, I was unsure whether the military could in fact put me in a cage with the prisoners. I didn't think that was how the Army operated.

Bradley, with whom I had established a special connection, had worked exclusively in Camps 1, 2, and 3 and so had participated in many ERFs. That night he and I sat for an extended period of time playing chess and talking about my first ERF. ERFs were common to Bradley, although he couldn't stomach them any better than I. He and I were both interested in learning things from the prisoners, and saw through the brainwashing and lies we had been told throughout training. We agreed we were both tired of the culture undermining daily interactions with the prisoners; our friendship grew stronger. We were already buddies; we would hang out with each other when time permitted. That night things changed between the two of us as I began to open up and talk about how I felt that what we were doing was just plain wrong. I talked about how I thought that maybe some of these people were innocent. As dangerous as this type of talk was inside the Army base, my trust in Bradley was well founded. I was taking a big chance saying anything like this out loud, but something told me I could trust him.

When we discussed what work had been like for me in the first three months in Camps 1, 2, and 3, I began to see it all differently. Bradley, in turn, voiced certain recognition when I talked about my work in Camp 4 and how pleasant and peaceful it had been for me when I started work. He confided in me that he'd had similar feelings, but felt that some of mine were on the extreme end of things. The conversation began a string of others that took place at the end of each shift. Sharing our stories and thoughts of what we had seen and heard helped us both get through the hours of each workday.

During this time (after my first ERF and the blatant fraternization that followed) I was growing increasingly uncomfortable. With only Bradley to talk to about what was happening, I felt alone. I would have talked with my wife about things, but phone conversations were monitored, as well as all internet usage. If either party said anything that infringed on OPSEC, the call would end. That would be it for the week, and soldiers had only one call per week to speak to loved ones.

Of slight comfort, though, was the fact that if a particular guard was rude and offensive to a prisoner in Camp 4, that same guard would be the object of retaliation, of the kind that only those with little else than the matter their own bodies produce can perform. That the prisoners had enough left in them to push back gave me a kind of inner hope that what we were putting these prisoners through would not totally destroy their souls. For acting out like this, recreation, shower time, soap and toothpaste would be taken away from a prisoner—and they would do it anyway, believing the punishment was worth the crime.

One late night, I made a goal: the next day I would have three questions answered; a) Who or what is a 'general'? (I didn't yet know), b) Where could I find a clear and coherently rendered set of protocols defining mission objectives? and c) Why did only the JIF interrogators speak Arabic in a place where over seven hundred prisoners did? Having prepared some Arabic flashcards, I jogged to chow hall the next morning while practicing the different greetings, questions, commands and phrases.

"Hello, how are you this morning, today, tonight?", "I need you to please sit down", "How do you say___ in Arabic?", "Can you stand against the wall with hands extended please?", and even the irrelevant, "Is the food okay?" were phrases I had thought of to try and make the unbearable bearable. I wanted to convey an idea not found in the words themselves: I want life to be as easy as possible here, for both of us.

I put my flashcards in my pocket, fixed the two-way on my shoulder, and went through the sally-port, greeting the officer at the end of the block and nodding to the two MPs on duty. We served everyone breakfast and began walking the block: up and down, up and down. I couldn't wait to use my newfound linguistic knowledge. In those higher-security camps, there seemed fewer English speakers among the prisoners, so I took the initiative to deal with translation personally. It could take as much as an hour to get simple tasks accomplished due to the language barrier. I wanted to see if it would be easier to get another prisoner to translate for me, or to teach myself enough to accomplish what needed to be done. Some of the prisoners would not only translate for me, but also teach me the Arabic alphabet—still others would teach me vocabulary.

This particular morning I walked up and down the block, my well-meaning flashcards in my pocket, ready to have a good day. I heard the echo of radios and people talking. When I came to the end of the hall, I turned and joined the group. I recognized one of my MP friends on duty, Pvt. Michael. There was also Smitty, who had already demonstrated a dislike for me, which was reciprocated.

"What's going on?" I asked Smitty.

Even though we were five feet from each other, Smitty answered into his two-way, "We're escorting a detainee from ISO into JIF care, Private Dumb-a**." This reflected Smitty's nature; he was simply a small-minded person, a sad little man. He cultivated friendships only with those exactly like him, which constituted a quarter of the guards working at GTMO—those who were just plain evil.

We opened the cell door and went inside. The prisoner (who I only knew by his number) wore a patchy neck-beard and was shorter than both of us. I quickly inspected the bunk, glanced over him, and prepared to put the chains on his feet through the port at the bottom of the metal-mesh barrier.

I was about to escort him to JIF when the familiar call to prayer blasted through the camps again, like clockwork.

When the prisoner fell to his knees in prayer on his prayer mat, Smitty exploded. "Get up! Damn it, get up right now." The prisoner's copy of the Quran was sitting close by and Smitty grabbed it and smacked the top of the prisoner's head while the man was in sujood. "Damn it, get up! I'm tired of hearing that damn noise every day. Doesn't it get boring for y'all? Same song or poem everyday makes a man insane, so get up or this book goes in the damn toilet where you squat every day, General. Do you hear me?"

The prisoner continued to pray, now out loud, "Sami' Allahu liman Hamida. (Allah hears the one who praises Him) Rabbanaa wa lakal Hamd (Our Lord, to You is all praise)." Into the toilet went the Quran, and Smitty kicked the lever. Private Michael picked it out of the toilet with a disgusted look on his face, quickly shackling the prisoner who had now broken his prayer due to the distraction.

"Damn it, Smitty. I was having a good day," Private Michael grumbled.

The prisoner was escorted out of his cell. I heard shouting from the other prisoners who had seen or heard what happened. The prisoner directly across the way was shouting down the hall at the others causing a near riot, saying something I interpreted as 'Infidels don't respect Islam!', or 'Infidels mock God!' It was the Jumuah—the Friday prayer—that Smitty had ruined for the prisoner.

The disruption in the camp ended quickly, and we escorted the prisoner to interrogation. During that somber march to JIF, I began to realize the older guards were affected, either due to their longer time at GTMO or their common mentality. Guys like Smitty, SSG Johnsville, and Sgt. Parks were nearly always the ones to blame when some kind of belligerent intolerance occurred. I saw Smitty eventually deface some copies of the Quran. Parks had the habit of turning off water to prisoners' cells. ERF's on SSG Johnsville's watch became commonplace. While doing my job I observed it, but when not at work, I kept away from the others, avoiding the 'recreation' crowd in general.

The 'Trio' back in Camp 4—Ruhal, Shafiq Rasul, and Asif Iqbal—would always be willing to speak with me, furthering my knowledge of Islam. They would ask me questions meant to inspire thought in me, to make me wonder and question. I found it an excellent way for them to teach me not only about Islam, but also about myself, to question my motivation for work and for life. Without offering the answers first, they set me on a path of knowledge and enlightenment. I wasn't given a set of precepts to filter things through: they were simply surprised and delighted that I was interested in Islam. I did try to reach Chaplain Yee, but he seemed always to be busy when it came to talking to guards about Islam, so I resorted to the library we had on base, finding some additional books to go with the Quran I had been given.

Surprise and delight would surely come to the prisoners, as I was one of a very few guards that did not take pleasure in insulting their religion. I did not delight in making it difficult for them to practice Islam. I was genuinely interested, asking questions with neither sarcasm nor hateful words. I apportioned the other soldiers in GTMO thus: one-quarter of them treated the prisoners like human beings, half were indifferent to the prisoners, and another quarter were pure evil. Tactics of humiliation and torture occurred at the hands of these types (and their superiors) that would win in any international torture contest. It was a constant source of disillusionment for me, hearing what would happen to the prisoners in interrogation. Those prisoners of which I was most fond (often those with the most knowledge of Islam and the world) would often receive the harshest treatment. Such prisoners had often been labeled 'generals' by these guards, arrogantly annoyed that a prisoner had the audacity to speak English and, not uncommonly, better English than they.

The tactics used on those prisoners seen as having significant knowledge had to be more sinister, as we prevented them from interacting with the general population after interrogations. So the misery that those prisoners went through could not be shared, even for comfort's sake, which no doubt made bearing it harder for them. If they were allowed to walk among the other prisoners after being water-boarded, sexually humiliated, confined in devices with insects, or following any number of other equally inhumane abuses, those running GTMO would have a riot on their hands.

Many prisoners were part of the 'frequent flier program': moved intermittently from block to block and cell to cell to deprive them of sleep and mental stability. A creative tactic of the JIF, it was used to draw more information from the prisoners. The results of interrogating those who had suffered this way had to have been largely useless.

A frequent victim of the 'frequent flier program', Ahmed Errachidi became psychotic in the spring of 2004 and was prescribed anti-psychotic drugs, but his interrogations continued: this resulted in disclosures ('information') that he was Jesus Christ, that Osama bin Laden was his student, and that a giant snowball was about to envelop the earth. The JIF apparently just selected whatever information suited their purposes.

I never directly observed torture and abuse, other than what I witnessed during ERFs. I certainly heard a great deal about it from suffering prisoners and boasting guards alike. Of course my job, especially in Camps 1, 2 and 3, required escorting prisoners to their interrogators. One such incident took place in September of 2003. We were asked to take a prisoner from his cell to an interrogation. The prisoner was older and unable to move as quickly as a younger man, and was duly punished for it. As we were shackling him, my partner told me to apply the shackles tighter, and then another guard reached in and clamped them down onto the skin so tightly that it must have caused great discomfort for the prisoner. We then began to walk him from the cell to the end of the block, and out of the sally-port. At GTMO, we had 'Gators' (off-road vehicles we used when taking a prisoner a long distance). As we began taking the prisoner to the vehicle, another guard got annoyed with how long it was taking. He thought he might step on the chain connecting the prisoner's ankles to motivate him to speed up.

This caused him to fall to the ground. Compressed so tightly by the shackles, his skin ripped as they ground into his flesh. I immediately tried to help the prisoner from the ground.

"Holdbrooks, f*** him," the guard yelled at me. "Get his lazy a** off the ground and let's get him moved already! The damn dirt farmer smells like my bowel movement earlier today." I was embarrassed and sincerely hoped that the prisoner understood no English. Ignoring his instructions, I helped him up anyway, and tried to even lift him a little as we walked so that he could move faster to avoid any more abuse from the other guard. We eventually got him to the Gator and transported him to the JIF, where he was shackled to a chair as we were told to leave the room.

"You really need to stop feeling sorry for these rag heads," the guard said to me as we exited the building. "They are the enemy, did you forget that? Each one of them is guilty. Each one of them hates America, hates freedom, and hates you." We made our way to the DOC building to get our next assignment, but as it turned out we didn't have that much to do that day. We went to the interrogation building to escape the heat. Unbeknownst to the interrogators, we witnessed some of what was going on.

In one room, a prisoner had been shackled to the ground, a strobe light in front of his face, the AC unit turned down to forty degrees Fahrenheit, with some awful music playing so loud it would cause deafness. He had been in the position so long that he had defecated on himself. The interrogator came in yelling, pouring cold water on him.

"Oh, how manly you are! Babies s*** themselves! Is that what you are? Do you need a diaper?"

I looked into another room where a prisoner was simply being questioned in what appeared to be a civilized manner, sitting in a chair with a Big Mac in front of him. They exchanged words as if they were just two human beings engaged in conversation. My partner and I found a room that was not being used, and laid down in there to cool off. Our rest was cut short after ten minutes, when we got a call over the radio to report to DOC.

"Here you go guys, looks as if you are taking the same detainee back to his cell already," the DOC officer said to us. We headed into the interrogation room and the interrogator confirmed that he was done so we should take him back to his cell. We started the process of taking him back to his cell, which included my partner dragging the prisoner in the dirt and telling him how badly he smelled. The prisoner could do nothing about his state of cleanliness: he was not free to shower when he liked, only when Camp operations permitted it. As for walking fast, this is difficult for anyone wearing shackles, let alone an injured, elderly man. Being low in rank, I had no other option than to try and make things as easy as possible. When we finally got him back to his cell, the other guard made a report to the block sergeant while I removed the absurdly tight shackles. Embarrassed by the whole trip and my inability to stop the abuse that it contained, I apologized to the prisoner.

"I am so sorry, please do not hate me." The prisoner was silent. He may not have understood English. He may not have been able to decide how to respond, but he did look at me in a very peculiar way. It was then time for a smoke break.

"You are not in Camp 4 anymore. You cannot be nice to the detainees," the other guard explained to me. "Just get the job done. At the end of the day, it doesn't make a difference if you are nice or mean. All that matters is that we get the mission done. You're not here to make friends, you're here to guard America from these sh**bags, and that is all we need to do, you copy?"

"Sure," I said, taking a heavy drag off my Marlboro.

After witnessing the kinds of things that happened in interrogations, I began to understand what was occurring at the JIF. This made it more difficult for me each time I had to escort a prisoner there. Stress positions, blaring music, ice cold rooms, screaming and such abuses were routine. The use of certain disturbing tactics—such as showing photos of dead women and children to a prisoner and then telling him it was his family, or playing sounds of a woman screaming while being raped and telling him it was his wife—were all sanctioned methods of interrogation. 'Acceptable' also included punching or kicking

71

prisoners as a form of 'attention grabbing'. It was not uncommon to see prisoners in stress positions which caused muscle failure and loss of bowel control, and then having to endure further abuse for being unable to endure that.

What is this? What are we doing? I would often think to myself. *Where was this getting us? Needlessly stepping on the hands, feet and heads of men during ERFs is not going to build us a great and powerful nation. Putting their faces in toilets and flushing it cannot be helpful towards any goal. Using a man's head to open a door instead of your own hand, is this really necessary?*

I found, of course, that these abuses only created more problems. Upset and angry, word of their abuse would spread quickly among the prisoners following an incident. When one guard named Sgt. Parks would conduct an ERF, he would to try induce fear in prisoners as he went rushing in. "YEE-haw, Camel Jockey, here I come!" he would holler as he went running in, sometimes without even a shield or riot gear. To beat a defenseless man and declare loudly, "I just got one for America," does not make you a man, a patriot or a good soldier.

After the incident with the elderly man, we got another call from DOC to pick up a different prisoner from the same block. I was worried about seeing the elderly man again, or seeing anyone else to whom he may have spoken about his injuries and insults. We walked onto the block, and a prisoner in the third cell called to me.

"MP, MP, hey you MP, come here," the prisoner called, and although it was not my task to take care of what was going on with that block, I stopped nonetheless. The prisoner continued, "You wait here." I looked at him, confused, as orders generally came from the guards to the prisoners and not the other way around.

"I cannot wait here, I have to go get another detainee and take him to interrogation," I explained. As I spoke, I heard the other guard—already down the block—begin to yell in revolt, disgust and anger at the few prisoners who had just showered him with feces and urine as he walked past.

"We know you good, good MP. You were not need to have that on you. Now go away quickly, before the others look," the prisoner who had stopped me advised.

That was how GTMO operated. When someone treated a prisoner as badly as my partner had, he was going to be punished for it. When one was compassionate, or even just as civil as I had been, he would be fine. I learned later on that the prisoner that my partner had been so rough with had told the others on the block what had happened, making it a point to explain that I was trying to be helpful and sympathetic during the process. Thus, I was spared from walking through the excrement shower. The prisoners were recognizing that I was not like these other guards. Perhaps word had gotten to them from Camp 4, or perhaps it was the simple, seemingly futile gestures of compassion I had demonstrated that morning.

My attitude was both a blessing and a curse. While the relationship that I wanted to establish between the prisoners and myself was made easier when they realized I was sympathetic to them, it imperiled me among my fellow guards and made life inside the camp increasingly dangerous.

The Professor

His face directly in the fan, Smitty looked ridiculous in the Cuban heat, refusing to dress down his BDU even a little. Smitty adhered to his own kind of protocol, as was apparent when he addressed me through his two-way when we were mere feet apart. Part of that protocol dictated that he would not dress down his BDU no matter what, no matter how hot it was at work. He stood talking one day with the block sergeant, and leaned over the sergeant's shoulder to hear the radio, letting the fan blow in his face.

He was talking to the sergeant as the sergeant spoke into a phone. The sergeant then hung-up and began walking towards Bradley and I. Trying to avoid Smitty, I slowly moved towards the exit, saying that I was going to the chow hall for a smoke break. Smitty motioned with his hand, speaking before the sergeant even had a chance.

"Yeah, you guys can go smoke after you escort Mr. Ahmed-whatever-Abdullah here to JIF interrogation, man," he said.

His work spoken for him by Smitty, the officer went back with Smitty to the officer's booth and continued talking about something I couldn't hear. Only Smitty's high-pitched laughter made it to my ears. I recognized the prisoner we had to escort to the JIF: his name was Ahmed. He was one of the penitent looking prisoners who was thumbing prayer beads and laughing at Ruhal's singing when I had arrived at GTMO.

We shackled Ahmed's hands and feet and escorted him to the JIF interrogation, where the interrogators took custody of him. Bradley and I were instructed to wait at the end of a long hallway while Ahmed went through a round of questioning, and whatever else they put him through. Thirty-five minutes later Ahmed emerged, his clothes and hair soaking wet. I was bewildered as to how that could have happened, short of having been doused in water. JIF handed the prisoner back over to us, and then Ahmed said he needed to use the restroom.

I opened the bathroom door and let him go in. Five minutes later, Ahmed popped his head out the door and said in Arabic, "The toilet's not working."

"It isn't? Open the door and step against the wall while I look at it," I replied in Arabic. So I stepped into the bathroom and the toilet was overflowing, soiled water everywhere. Bradley moved Ahmed towards the wall nearest the door while I took a look at the toilet. I took the top off to try to stop the water flow, but that didn't work. I then reached behind the toilet to turn off the water mains, and turned the stubborn knob until I heard the water slam to a halt in the wall behind me. I had my head turned, and when I looked down I saw I'd knocked a piece of paper loose. It had been wedged between the knob and the water main. With Bradley and Ahmed outside speaking to JIF about the water mess, I quickly unfolded the paper and gazed in wonder at what I saw: a map!

Well-drawn, it had a large portion of the Camp Delta layout mapped. It was marked to size using what looked like footsteps or half-yards as the scale. The map had different people's names marked in each camp, as well as intricate religious drawings. Beautiful calligraphy and great artistry decorated this paper, discovered behind a toilet. I realized that giving it to the JIF would result in Ahmed being interrogated for hours afterwards, Bradley and myself being debriefed, and the DOC making 'much ado about nothing'. I stuffed the map in my boot and carried on.

We escorted Ahmed back to his block and let him into his cell. Smitty walked over from the guard's shack.

"Damn, Private, you look like you pissed all over yourself and your prisoner on the way there," he teased. In trying to turn off the water, clean water from the tank had gotten on my BDU. I opened my mouth to reply, but thought better of it and stopped myself. Bradley planted his two-way in my hand and jogged off so he could go smoke or get lunch, leaving me to follow Smitty around.

It was so hot that by the time Bradley got back a half-hour later, my BDU was bone-dry. I almost told him about the map, but decided to wait. Instead, I invited him over to my condo for chess later that night.

That evening, Bradley knocked on the door. I put down my copy of 'Islam for Dummies', and came downstairs to let him in. We moved to the living room and Bradley set up the chessboard while I brewed coffee in the kitchen.

"Bradley, did you see Smitty today? I can't believe he doesn't dress down his BDU; he was wetter than me most of the afternoon."

Bradley sat cross-legged in the living room, looking at the chess pieces that were lined up perfectly. "Yeah...Smitty, Park and Johnsville have all been acting weird lately. They are planning something sinister. I heard Smitty on the phone with Parks or Johnsville, or someone else on his softball team, talking about looking for 'sluggers' to rig a game, or something desperate like that."

I poured two cups of coffee and walked into the living room, handed Bradley his mug and sat down at the other end of the chessboard. "Well, that whole group is sinister; it wouldn't surprise me if they like a rigged game. It's pretty sad they cheat when they play against each other, though."

I lit a cigarette and leaned back into my beanbag chair, hands behind my head. Holding my cigarette between my lips I said to Bradley, trying to make it seem like a joke to test the waters, "Yeah, man, there's something wrong with this whole damn operation." I reached behind me and put a mixed CD into the entertainment center. What played was System of a Down's song "Inner Vision": it was a compromise for us because, unlike me, Bradley liked gangster rap.

I started our game with the traditional and risky French opening I'd read about in my chess strategy book. It advances the pawns defending the king and queen first. Bradley advanced his pawns on the left (in front of his rook) and came after me, falling right into my trap. We played until Bradley had taken one of my bishops, by which point I had his rooks. I took the last sip of coffee, now cold, before getting up to pour myself more.

When I returned, I was carrying my boots, which I set down beside me.

Bradley was staring intently at the chessboard when I sat down. I imagined he was wondering how he could still win at least this small game as he was powerless to make anything else happen the way he wanted it to.

"Bradley, I want to show you something," I said.

"Come on, Holdbrooks, I'm concentrating. I'll read your chess-book later."

I took the map out of my boot, unfolded it and handed it to Bradley. "I'm sure this is why Ahmed couldn't wait to piss. I found it behind the toilet while I was getting soaked from that tank spouting water."

Bradley looked at the map for a second and responded, "A map? There's a good deal of Uyghur calligraphy on here man. Are you sure that Ahmed was writing this?"

"No, no Bradley. It's obviously a collaborative, man. Look at the drawings of all the camps, look at the names, and aliases and drawings. This was some kind of work in progress with footsteps to keep the whole thing to scale."

Looking again at the map, Bradley said, "The name 'Shaker' and 'Imam' is written on here at least once in each drawn camp, except Iguana, like he's everywhere or something."

I unfolded the bottom portion of the map, turning it around. Doing this revealed a talented depiction of an aging, mysterious-looking, emaciated person, wearing a turban, sitting cross-legged, pointing up towards the calligraphy at the top of the page. It read in Arabic, 'Glory be to Allah, the One Almighty God, and His Prophet Muhammad (Peace be upon him)'. I then folded the map back together and put it into my pocket.

"Anyone could have written that: all the detainees know about the Professor. I feel sorry for him, man. He looks scrawnier and more rugged each time I see him lately, like he hasn't slept in weeks or something. But he's a real polite man, even when I have to wake him at 0300 for the frequent flier program," Bradley commented.

Between taking Bradley's queen and sacrificing my second bishop to put him in checkmate, I decided that I should try to get to know the Professor the next chance I was given. I wanted to surprise him by answering in Arabic the questions he would ask about his friends.

Bradley and I went outside and lit the miniature barbeque grill on the ground. We threw a few hamburgers on it, and sat on the plastic patio chairs. The only light was the barbeque between us; I took the map out of my pocket, poking it into the coals. I couldn't have that found in my possession. The fire glowed brighter. I sat closer to it and looked at Bradley.

"Man, I don't know what we're doing here, or how I'm going to get through being a part of it, but I know I need something new, something bigger than myself or my marriage to not f***ing lose it," I admitted out loud.

Bradley didn't say a word through dinner. He took my chess strategy book, thanked me and promptly left. That was his way.

The decorated paper map was in fact a kind of homemade newspaper that the prisoners had organized amongst themselves. One was writing it, or dictating what it would state, while another was producing the calligraphy, with a final adding art to the sides for aesthetics. I found another map later, in the pages of a Quran. I had to turn this one in, though, as there was no way for me in that circumstance to hide my discovery. It too was a marvel of artistry and calculation. The mapmaker had an accuracy measurement of the camp to nearly 25 feet. He was able to do this, as I later discovered, by measuring the distance of a step he could take with his shackles on, and then using that to determine how long a block was, which lead him to learn how large a Camp was. This particular prisoner had been moved around so much that he had toured more than half of Camp Delta, calculating each step.

Since this map was confiscated, the prisoner who drew it created another (quite soon) from memory, and was subsequently put into the isolation block for doing so. My leaders never said a word to me about this incident, but swift action was taken as we were told to search more cells more often, moving prisoners around all the time. After the discovery of these drawings which, for some time, had gone completely unnoticed by guards and interrogators alike, the isolation blocks filled up quickly.

After my conversation with Bradley, I went to bed that night thinking about my wife. For the first time since I'd arrived at GTMO, I felt no comfort from the thought of her love. She was becoming a cliché—imaginary—in my mind. The 'American-dream' lifestyle that she now evoked was in my mind a cruel, teasing joke. After working at a place like this, I could never return to the innocence and naivety we had shared in our decision to marry. As for the separation anxiety, the only relief from that were the weekly fifteen-minute phone calls, but they weren't reducing my misery, not even incrementally.

The next morning, I woke up, got dressed and went to work. I started walking the block, addressing a few of the prisoners. The Professor was on our block that day for the first time in weeks; he lay sleeping while I watched the block. I started to notice some new MP faces on the block that day including Sgt. Parks (who normally worked in Camp 3, or sat around all day eating lunch with his other Regime buddies).

I probably should have realized then that others in my company were getting new assignments, while I was not. Preoccupied by my weakening morale, I had much more important things on my mind than promotion or varied assignments. I instead put my energies into trying to be inconspicuous, so as not to be seen by Parks speaking Arabic to the prisoners. I didn't want to have to explain to Parks that speaking their dialect didn't make me a traitor, it just made life easier. In fact, the silence between us often grew awkward, so whenever we were on duty together I usually managed to find an excuse to talk with prisoners and get away from him for a short time.

Parks didn't need to say much to let me know that he disliked me because I didn't play soft-ball after work, chew tobacco all day, or belligerently abuse the prisoners. We both realized soon enough that we were nothing alike; our loathing of one another was thinly veiled.

As time passed, it began to grow cooler outside; the afternoon storms that rolled in every day cooled things off nicely. I grabbed a few blankets from the guard shack and stepped outside. I walked to the end of the block and turned around. I stayed until the other guards were sitting with Parks, waiting until the silence was inevitably awkward, and then left to deliver blankets to the prisoners.

About twelve steps later, to my right, was the Professor. He was no doubt the one depicted on the map/newspaper as the emaciated, pious man. I had not yet had the opportunity to cultivate a connection with him, as he never remained very long in one place at the camp. He was on the frequent flier program.

I had known who the Professor was from week one at GTMO. Three months into my stay, I would see him sleeping when I arrived for my shift, or talking with other prisoners. I had also escorted him a few times, late at night. While I remembered hearing him speak English to other prisoners, I had never spoken to him myself, nor answered him when he addressed me about his complaints, beliefs, or the problems of other prisoners. I was usually on duty with Smitty, who would sooner yell at prisoners to shut up 'till he was red in the face rather than actually address their problems with any degree of civility or professionalism.

This time, however, the Professor was awake and not in conversation with anyone. He was smearing what looked like feces onto the very top portion of the small slit of the window in his cell. I chose to address him in Arabic.

"What are you doing?" I inquired.

He turned around and put the fingers he was smearing with into his mouth, and then laughed at my look of surprise. He had a large beard, and carried too little weight for a man with such a big frame.

"It is peanut butter from the MREs. I kept it folded inside my uniform. The sun melts the butter and separates the oil. It's good for treating rashes and the bruises from being shackled in awkward positions for ten or eleven hours at a time."

81

I recognized the bruises on his hands, as they were similar to those of other prisoners I'd escorted from JIF back to Delta. The bruises came from squatting, hands shackled behind the legs to force one to remain in the stressed position.

The Professor spoke at least six languages and perfect English. He was articulate, humble, and surprisingly well adjusted to the activities at GTMO: abuses, the frequent interrogations, and excessive isolation. He was smart enough to know the only thing he could do about the situation was not get upset, continuing his hunger strike and seeking refuge in the almighty Allah.

"Why not go to medical?" I asked, knowing we had excellent medical services on base to treat the injuries.

Smiling, the Professor answered, "They always try and get me to eat something."

The Professor's hunger strike was what he had left in terms of initiative; he hoped it would draw attention to the abuses and the unjust incarceration. He looked considerably thinner than the husky man I had seen months before. His cheekbones were protruding and his chest had sunken in. Looking down at the end of the camp, I saw Sgt. Parks put a huge wad of chewing tobacco in his mouth, staring directly at me as I continued speaking with the Professor. I handed the Professor his extra blankets. Parks turned around and put his feet up on the desk in the officer's pen. Again, I addressed the Professor.

"Do you think it's possible to be a good Muslim in prison?"

Surprised, the Professor asked back, "Are you a Muslim, my brother?"

"I am not a Muslim, but recently I've started to feel like God might be what I'm missing in my life."

The Professor replied in Arabic, "Allah is always present in our lives. What's missing is our will to submit to His Divine Wisdom and Forgiveness for our trespasses." His words might have struck a deeper note in my heart if it had not been for the noise of Parks' echoing laughter, other prisoners yelling to each other about the MREs, and spasmodic announcements blaring over the loudspeakers. What a bizarre and unexpected place to reach a religious epiphany.

"I don't know, as I've never been religious. I've struggled with faith my entire life," I answered.

The Professor smiled yet again. "I struggle with faith, but I remember my children, I remember my students, and I remember my brothers here in GTMO...they are my strength, so I'm strong for them, strong for Allah." He was strong, I understood, because he was a respected elder here. If he folded or sank into despair, then others would too. The situation could become even more utterly hopeless for everyone else around him if he gave into misery or self-pity. Another question occurred to me.

"So how do good Muslims, scholars, fathers, and teachers end up here?"

The Professor responded by telling me a bit about who he was and about the circumstances surrounding his incarceration at GTMO. He was a father of four, a Saudi Arabian citizen and charity worker who was abducted in Afghanistan while working for the Saudi "Al-Haramain Foundation". This foundation or charity was suspected of diverting some of its funds to the Taliban.

He told me that he was gravely worried about his wife, whose mental decline had been steady since he had left her and their four children. His story up to this point had been told in Arabic, but now he looked me in the eyes, speaking in English.

"I am an innocent man who misses his wife and children. I had never heard of Al-Qaeda until it was on the news, until I came here." The Professor took a few steps back and sat down on his bunk, breathing a heavy sigh. He started unfolding his new blanket, in reality a comfort item in this area of the camp. I offered some personal disclosure in return, although small in comparison. Ignoring the glare of Sgt. Parks, I leaned forward.

"I have a wife, too."

"Then you know how I feel, separated from her for over three years now. I pray to Allah every day to cure her madness, and to cure the madness this place has infected me with. Tell me, I haven't seen Ruhal or Ahmed in a while. Do they still live here, or are they gone? Allah forbid, they are by themselves in isolation again?"

"Ruhal's not in isolation. His friends are around here somewhere. Ruhal is hilarious—in good spirits—not just reciting Quran, but singing songs to entertain his friends too," I informed him. Laughing a bit, which induced further coughing, the Professor refolded his blanket and got up to hand it to me.

"You know, I've grown pretty accustomed to the weather here, maybe you should take my blanket." Taking the blanket, I felt that something was wrapped inside. I turned and walked back towards the guard shack, feeling inside the blanket and noticing the edge of a book concealed within. I realized the Professor had given me his copy of the Quran. Unable at this point to remove it and bring it with me, I returned the blanket to the cubby from which I had taken it.

"Well, didn't he want the blanket?" Sgt. Parks asked, bringing his feet from the top of the desk to rest on the ground.

"No, he didn't want the blanket or lunch today," I replied. Parks unlocked the guard shack to step outside, pausing.

"Guy doesn't want food, doesn't want a blanket, doesn't want anything but to be free to blow people up again," Parks said as he gazed down the hallway. He looked back at me and continued, "Someday you're gonna learn these people aren't worth the spit you waste talking to them, Private." I smiled apathetically. Parks let the door to the guard shack slam shut, spitting a nasty gob of Copenhagen onto the ground as he mumbled something to himself, and strolled out of Camp 3 (and, thankfully, out of my world for the next two days). The next time I would see him would be on 'mandatory fun day', at the softball game that was to begin changing things around GTMO.

Fun in the Sun

If I had played ball, figuratively and literally, and hung around those in my unit more, discussing women, sports, music or video games (or taken part in the other social activities), I might not have been singled out. If I had joined in their insults and abuse and visible hatred of the prisoners, my loyalty would not have been questioned. Obviously I didn't, nor did I participate in such displays, so I found company in myself and Bradley, who was the only one I could talk with about feelings, thoughts, politics, social views, or ethics. Nothing of substance and value could be discussed with the larger population of soldiers I worked with. Even if they felt drawn to converse with me about any of that, being seen talking to me was tantamount to being like me: a sympathizer, a traitor.

"Holdbrooks, are you an American!?" my squad leader SSG Johnsville asked me one day.

"Well, of course I am SSG. I am in the Army, serving my country," I replied.

"Then why the f*** do you care what these people think, how they feel, how they speak or what they believe?! You need to pull your head out of your a** and get with the program. We are here to guard America from the terrorists that want to harm us, and these detainees are all terrorists. They all hate us! Don't you ever forget that!" he answered. Many similar conversations would take place with Johnsville and my team leader Sgt. Nord, and then the temporary team leader, Sgt. Parks.

At first, I clung to the faint hope that deep down, my superiors felt as I did. I had hoped that behind the shouting and harsh words, they were merely relaying that they had a job to do—that their concern was the mission—that my behavior was counterproductive in their view. I didn't want to recognize that my superiors shared the same hateful mentality as those who worked closely with me. It would have been more than I could bear, the recognition that what I was thinking and feeling were opposite that of nearly everyone around me, trapped as I was in that armpit of the world. I tried to adapt to the new working context I found myself in, under scrutiny and suspicion. I was no longer in the frying pan, but directly in the fire itself.

In an effort to clear my mind and come to grips with my fragile situation, I did a little off-camp exploring. I spent time at a beach near the chow hall by Camp Delta. I went by the facility where the child prisoners were held, Camp Iguana. Every time I passed by there, I could not help but reflect over how unfathomable it was that holding children captive would help.

At times I would be stopped by armed guards, telling me the beach was off-limits. I thought it was because I'd arrived at the same time that the children were granted swim time once a week. No direct interaction with the children at Camp Iguana was allowed, except for those working there, so I never knew how they were treated, which just added to my misery and regret.

I explored the whole island. One day, I came across another facility, but a guard pointed his gun at me and told me to leave. Again, putting two and two together I assumed that it was where Khalid Sheikh Mohammed and the other valuable prisoners were held: the infamous Camp No. It was called Camp No because, when the COC was questioned about whether it existed, its name was the answer. Camp No must have been where prisoners were water-boarded, confined in coffins with insects, and made to endure other horrible things that have since come out in the media, as interrogators could not do that to someone and then release him in the general population. There would be retaliation.

At another point in time, during some land navigation training, my squad came upon what looked like older facilities, dating back to World War II, possibly even earlier. It made me wonder: *How long have we been using GTMO as a place of torture and detainment? During how many conflicts have we used this soil to wrongly hold people? Were the Japanese held here during World War II, and the Koreans or Vietnamese after them?* It is not likely to end soon. The agreement states that both parties have to agree to end the lease, and although Cuba repeatedly tries to do so, the United States will not return the tiny scrap of island to them.

The nightly chess games between Bradley and I were symbolic of what was happening in the bigger picture at GTMO. It began to dawn on me that we were all participating in a type of chess game, where we were all pawns, moving singularly. The Army lived with Army, MPs lived with MPs, and headquarters lived with headquarters. The Marines kept to themselves, as did the Navy and Air Force. Even the infantry soldiers who guarded GTMO against adversaries or prevented prisoner escapes didn't talk to anyone else. At GTMO, there were no inter-branch or inter-job relations. My senior leaders were allotted just enough information about the grand scheme to accomplish their mission and ensure its success. I slowly began to understand why we were all monitored and kept segregated. Each of us was given only enough knowledge to perform our daily tasks, without being informed about how we contributed to the larger picture or, in fact, what the larger picture was at all. Without people sharing information and establishing their own ties, the pawns were more easily moved about and manipulated.

This segregation was something passed down to GTMO from much higher up than just a two-star general. General Miller was a cipher of the DOD, because someone of his rank could not have orchestrated something on this scale of organization and mandate. It had to have come from someplace higher up. This segregation even prevented me from getting some tips on Arabic language for my studies, as even the linguists kept to themselves.

While sections of the DOD didn't interact, there was, although against the rules, a lot of fraternization between the people with whom I worked. For example, privates through privates first-class could fraternize, but officers were prohibited (at least on paper) from hanging around enlisted men. The Regime, however, included all ranks, and it shocked me how fraternization was a reward for the vicious behavior displayed. You could break the rules, if you broke with protocol. As bizarre as it was, it formed the brotherhood that was the Regime. The men in it had the same mentality about the prisoners as they did about me and my interests in Arabic and Islam. The Regime lived for 'mandatory fun day', binge drinking, boating and scuba diving, swearing and being violent, and they punished those who did not deign to share in their activities.

They were not authorities to whom decision-making power should have been granted. Regardless of official structure, the Regime was, in reality, running the unit. This clique of SSGs and sergeants was dictating who was working where in the camp, with whom, how often, and what work was being done. They had lost a moral compass guiding what it means to be an American—to be a soldier—much less how to accomplish the mission at hand. The mission was to take care of the day-to-day operations at GTMO: feed the prisoners, move them when needed, rotate for showers and recreation, take them to and from hospital, dentist, interrogation, etc. Contrary to the view of those in the Regime, the mission was not to disrespect the prisoners, belittle them, harm them or abuse them. This Regime would reward those who displayed aggression towards the prisoners, those who talked down to them or harmed them whenever possible. The COC was not present in the camp often enough to see what was going on, and out of fear no one of a lower rank would ever inform them of the Regime's stranglehold.

In one of our many conversations, Bradley and I were discussing the attitude of those in the Regime and the results of that in the day's atrocities.

"Speaking of needless suffering, you know we've got the day after tomorrow off for mandatory fun day, right?" Bradley said, changing the subject.

"Oh great, just what I want to do, spend more 'fun' time with Sgt. Parks and company. Who's scheduled to play softball?"

"I think our company's playing on the softball field and everyone else is either swimming or playing football. It's such garbage though, mandatory fun. Isn't that kind of redundant? 'Have fun, or else!' you know?" Bradley replied.

I could imagine worse things happening, but the list was pretty short. Bradley and I finished our second game of chess and Bradley walked home. The following day passed without incident: I spoke with the Professor and thanked him for the book, and after work went home and read the Quran by myself until I fell asleep with it by my side. The next day I woke up and walked to the PX area near the beach to meet my company for a 'mandatory fun' day of softball.

Even though the Regime didn't have the final word about scheduling the softball game, much less the institution of mandatory fun day, they seemed to manipulate the situation well enough to their advantage. It was their way of castigating those who weren't 'participating' in life outside the prison—those not playing softball with them every day.

The teams for the softball game that day were drawn from a hat. It would have been nice to have blamed the disparity on the Regime, as they couldn't have arranged it better if they had chosen the teams themselves. By the time everyone had drawn their straws, it became apparent that Team 2 was in for a major-league beating. Team 1 was basically composed of the Regime members: Smitty, Michael, Parks, and Johnsville—all notorious for late night boozing and abuses.

My first sergeant was the biggest hitter on our team. We had a few sluggers, but the rest of the team, myself included, had never played ball together. The Regime played ball together every single day. It was a recipe for disaster and, no doubt, a plebeian betting pool.

The small benches and grassy area were full of observers from the base. The first three innings went by without my team even getting a man past second. Every time we hit to infield, the other team fielded the ball so quickly that my first sergeant would get red in the face, yelling, "God d*** it boys! Don't let him make the tag! Go back! Go back!" Every time we hit to outfield, Team 1 caught the ball, to the enthusiastic and overwhelming applause of the observing company.

By the seventh inning my team hadn't scored a single run. That should have ended the game, but my first sergeant's pride wouldn't allow it. It was our turn to bat, and he was up. Pvt. Michael was the pitcher. He looked serious-as-hell, and it was clear he didn't have any intention of letting my first sergeant get even one hit. He threw four balls. Red in the face and swearing under his breath, the sergeant walked to first base.

I was somewhere far away in my mind when a hand slapped me on the back and one of my teammates said to me, "You're up, man. Good luck."

The score was 6-0 and the pressure was on. I picked up the bat from the sandy white dirt and knocked it against my shoes, watching as the small cloud of dirt flew off and headed east. I licked my finger and held it to the wind. *Yes, east for sure.* Facing Pvt. Michael, I stepped up to bat. Smitty was manning first base, Sgt. Parks on second, and SSG Johnsville on third. The last five and a half months of abuses at their hands flew through my mind in a vicious montage: I saw Smitty throwing a Quran in the toilet and flushing it, Sgt. Parks spitting Copenhagen into prisoners' faces, and Johnsville roaring insults as he ran to an ERF. I saw Ahmed soaking wet, half drowned and drained of his pride, and I saw the Professor emaciated, holding his hand up to give me his copy of the Quran, tears running down his face.

Whispering the words, "Insha-Allah" (God willing), I braced myself for Pvt. Michael's first pitch. I swung. I swung with everything I had—everything I wished could be—and the bat connected with the ball. Without knowing where the ball flew, I threw the bat and ran. Everyone else squinted into the bright sun to see where it was going. As I rounded first base, I heard Smitty.

"It's gone, Parks! Gone into the f***ing ocean, what do you know?!"

I didn't slow down in my run. My first sergeant got himself home, and so did I. We walked behind the fence and he patted me on the back. Winded, I managed to say, "Yeah, it's just too bad I had to wait until the end of the game to do that."

Putting his hat back on, with his hand on my shoulder, the sergeant said, "Private, I believe the real game has just begun around here."

Two innings later, the game ended 8-2. I walked back to the condos a few miles away, knowing there would probably be hell to pay for smacking that ball into the ocean. I smiled anyway, knowing Allah had worked through me, through my bat, praying that my own premonition wouldn't manifest itself.

The General

I hadn't spoken to my wife in some time. My disdain for GTMO was growing worse each day as the nature of the abuses grew worse. The prisoners in Camps 1, 2 and 3 were, of course, the most miserable at the base. My wife's voice and tender words no longer did anything to wash away—even for the allotted 15 minutes—the darkness that had settled on my heart. So I called her less and less.

The day after the softball game I woke up to a new day. I took the bus to the base, met my company for a quick morning meeting, and was issued my new assignment. Still assigned to Camps 1, 2, and 3, I was going to be working mid-shift. My new duties worked me odd hours of the day and night, giving me a much better chance to speak with prisoners.

While I had certainly heard of the prisoner nicknamed 'The General', I hadn't actually spoken with him. Because he was on the 'frequent flier' program, Ahmed Errachidi had been moved so frequently and at such late hours that I had not once seen him in the same time and place since I began work at GTMO.

Known on paper as 'Prisoner 590', he would certainly recognize me at this point, and I knew him as 'The General' by reputation. He was the prisoner that spoke perfect English and often proclaimed his innocence to guards when we served him meals. The other guards either ignored him or yelled at him to shut up when he would do this; I was different, especially after my third week working in Camp 2.

It was already dark outside and early into my shift as I served the prisoners' dinner. I went to the end of the block and saw Errachidi sitting cross-legged, reading the Quran.

"Dinner time," I announced.

Errachidi closed the book and walked up to the front of the cell mesh and spoke, eyeing me as he did so.

"How does it feel to serve an innocent man—a caged man—his food, American boy? I am innocent. Where are my basic human rights?"

I was taken aback. I couldn't remember the last time I'd been so directly confronted by a prisoner. I was completely surprised by Errachidi's disposition and perfect English. I replied to him in Arabic.

"Why should I believe you?"

"I have been tortured, kept awake for weeks, and starved. If I was your enemy, I would have proudly declared it by now."

"That's a real clever answer, man. You'll have to tell me all about it sometime." I replied, only half-joking. I wished I could physically shake off the feeling that his frank response threw at me. Unsmiling, Errachidi took his meal from me quietly. He nodded, looking at his food tray.

"Sometime."

A week later was the first time I recall having the impression that Errachidi was a revered figure at GTMO. I had already heard comments by the Professor and Ruhal, and also read things to that effect on the map I had found.

It was a month into my re-assignment; I was standing guard with Johnsville. It was late at night, a few hours after dinner. All the prisoners were at this time settling into their bunks to get some sleep.

Fifteen open windows let the light of the full, bright moon into the camp. The windows were spaced a few feet apart, high up on the back wall. They offered the only glimpse of the outside world that the prisoners had, aside from their hour of recreation each week. The light from the guard shack, my flashlight, and the moon were the only sources of light we had. If something went bump in the night, or something went wrong, we could always turn on the main lights, although it wasn't advisable.

That night I was walking the block, struggling to stay awake. I saw something that looked like a large ferret crawl

94

through the window at the opposing end of the block. To the guard nearest the guard shack, I whispered.

"Hey, man. What the hell was that?" The guard had obviously not seen the thing drop from the wall onto the floor. I repeated the question, a little louder now: "Hey! Hey man! What the hell was that was that thing!? Look!"

The MP turned around and saw the huge ferret-like thing scurrying towards the guard shack and the sally-port doors. He then responded in the most stupid way possible. He screamed like a little child.

"Aggh! What is it!?" the MP screamed. This woke up every prisoner that wasn't fully asleep. The MP rushed towards the beast as it zigzagged past him towards me. All the prisoners on the block saw it, whipping them all into a panic.

Everyone on the block began to shout at once. I ran over to SSG Johnsville and told him what was going on; he obviously wasn't concerned. A huge banana rat had covertly snuck into his block, and there he was, sitting listening to the radio. He merely suggested that I usher it out with a mop, and then reached over to call the guards to open the doors for it. I rushed over to the cleaning supply area, grabbing the huge mop I used each day, and then walked towards the rat. It was too huge and fat to scurry back up the wall from whence it came. A number of the prisoners were now screaming and crying in Arabic things like 'It's a monster!', and 'It's filthy, get it away!'

Not intimidated by me in the least, the banana rat didn't move. As I hit it with the mop, trying to direct it towards the door, a few prisoners started tossing in their bunks, swearing, and throwing themselves against their cell bars when the rat passed by their cells. It was fast becoming a very serious riot scene in which I feared the entire block would be dealt ERFs, sent to the ISO, or worse.

The rat zigzagged passed me at the end of the block by Errachidi's cell. I looked at Errachidi and he nodded: we both understood in that moment the severity of the situation. With Johnsville standing outside in the guard shack waiting for the rat to come running by and out the doors, Errachidi addressed the cellblock.

"My brothers, it is merely a vermin," he called out to them in Arabic, "Quiet your selves while they flush it out of our block."

Like magic, Errachidi's voice caused peace to settle on the prisoners as they quieted down to a whisper. Prisoners who moments before were in a full-scale panic were going back to bed. I walked double-time towards the rat, which was finally headed for Johnsville. Smacking it hard to stun it, I picked it up with the end of the mop and carried it outside. Johnsville stood there with a blank look as I passed him to go back down to the end of the block where Errachidi was held. I thanked him.

"Do you still think I am your enemy, boy?" Errachidi asked.

Intrigued and grateful, I arrived for work the following day. I spoke with Errachidi at length. He proclaimed his innocence again, but told me his story as well.

"In September 2001 I left London on a business trip to Pakistan to buy and sell silver. During my time in Pakistan there were horrific images coming out of Afghanistan. I was moved and devastated by what I saw. It was an emotional time for me because my son had heart problems back home. I decided to put my business venture on hold and cross into Afghanistan for a few days, to make a humanitarian aid contribution to the Afghan people.

"Once I arrived, I witnessed the horror and random killing of civilians. I had underestimated the extent of the problem and had made a mistake by going. It was impossible for me to return to Pakistan because of the bombings there. After 25 days I found a way out of Afghanistan with hundreds of other people who were also escaping the war. When I got to Pakistan, the car that I was traveling in was involved in a car accident; the accident was serious enough for the Pakistani Police to get involved. They arrested me, along with other passengers, and locked me up for forty-four days, during which I was interrogated by the FBI and the Pakistani Intelligence, both of whom promised me that they were going to send me home. But they lied to me and sold me to the U.S. Army for five-thousand American dollars. I then found myself in Baghram, then Kandahar, and eventually here at GTMO, where you and I met of course...

"The Americans accused me of receiving terrorist training in Afghanistan in July 2001 which, of course, was purely a lie because I had not left London before September 18th 2001; in July I was working as a cook in a Five Star Hotel in Mayfair, London. I have pay slips to prove it."

I stopped him there, as I had to get some work done before my shift came to an end. His story stayed in my mind. It was strikingly similar to the stories many prisoners had already told me. I was beginning to wonder what there was to be gained from all these men if they were, in fact, telling the truth. Later that shift I found more free time and Errachidi stopped me as I passed his cell, asking about my tattoos.

"Why have you marked yourself up so much like you have? Are you not proud of your temple? Your body is how Allah sees you, how he made you in your perfection."

The thought made me think about my tattoos, and so I knelt down and explained to him each one of them, and their meanings. I felt relieved that Errachidi could only see four of them.

"Well, you see," I explained, "each of these tattoos is a representation of some thought or struggle I have had in my life." As I explained to Errachidi how I was a product of my generation, and that tattoos were something commonplace and acceptable in America, I began to think about how my body was my temple, and contemplated about what I had indeed done to it.

"You see, these barbed wires around my wrists are symbolic of a wonderful girlfriend I had in the past who I cheated on one night when I was under the influence of prescription meds and alcohol. That doesn't excuse my behavior, but when I came to my senses the next day, I felt awful, and it was worse when I had to tell her, and see the look in her eyes. I remember clearly how guilty I felt, how low and awful I felt, how fundamentally loathsome. So in turn I went and got these tattooed on me the next day to remind me that I am taken, that my hands are imprisoned and to not let them get me into any further trouble." Not surprisingly, Errachidi looked confused, and then asked about the other tattoos, higher up on my arms.

"Well, those are simple. They represent the duality of man, something I have always thought of as being a joke really. The one on my right arm is Satan, and the one on my left is Jesus." Errachidi gasped.

"Peace be upon him," he added, as Muslims all do in a prayer mentioned at the names of all prophets of God.

"Why would you want to get the devil tattooed on you? In our faith to make an image of either is very wrong."

"That is exactly my point, in your faith it is wrong, and there is a duality conflict, which I do not believe in. I think we all have the ability to make our own decisions and there is no absolute evil or good," I countered, but was interrupted by Errachidi.

"There is an absolute good, which is the way of Allah: be like the Prophet, and live as he lived, and avoid Shaytan (Satan) at all costs." This began an argument that lasted some time. As time would pass, he would further explain that the nature of duality does exist in Islam, but is nowhere near as prevalent as it is in the Judeo-Christian society. Errachidi's response reflected my own feeling profoundly, despite having barely begun my Islamic studies.

"I will pray for your forgiveness," Errachidi said finally, leaving me to ponder why he would bother praying for me. *What made him care?*

On other occasions, Errachidi and I would have more in-depth, less confrontational dialogues. We would discuss history, government and politics, neither accusing the other of ever being wrong. Errachidi was a wise man, and his excellent grasp of English and conversation helped frame questions that would prompt ever-deeper inquiry from me. I eventually arrived at the realization that the worldview I previously had may be wrong, and I began to see truth for the first time in my life.

Of worry, however, was that sometimes Errachidi was not able to keep up with the conversation. I thirsted for more wise words from the prisoner that became my teacher, but the stress and torture he endured fatigued his body and his mind. His mental and cognitive faculties were questionable at times; at still other times he didn't even recognize me. *What was happening to him in interrogation that would so affect this intelligent and wise man?* I asked myself. In retrospect, I think I knew, but it was something too horrible to be recognized in a fully conscious way. Now that I was learning something interesting and new every day, I could see the how the darkness in this place was affecting my teacher, and it was something I could no longer brush aside with ease.

In addition to my meaningful conversations with Errachidi, I began to read the Quran more every day. I wanted a deeper understanding of Islam, to understand what the prisoners were all practicing. It had been a massive culture shock for me to see religion taken so seriously. I had held the idea for too long that faith in anything was laughable. I was used to witnessing people adhere more faithfully to their choice in music or their favorite sports team than their religion. Here were all these men, falsely imprisoned with no rights, and they were still adhering to their faith, with their situation prompting more strength of conviction than ever before.

I asked myself many questions in a willed effort to block the obvious sincerity and unity of purpose the prisoners demonstrated: *Was it because this was all they had? Was it because they peer-pressured each other?* It became clear that their religion was all they really needed and, similarly, that spiritual answers were needed for the questions arising in my soul.

Somehow Chaplain Yee didn't mind answering questions from the prisoners, but never seemed to have time when it came to answer my questions about Islam. So it came to be that from the prisoners I received spiritual insights. They were all more than willing to answer any questions I had, and also to suggest other books, and encourage me to ask again. Continuing my discussions with the prisoners about Islam, I repeatedly observed that even in this horrible place, with all the miserable things perpetrated on them daily, what kept the smiles on their faces was Islam. I wondered where my own smile had gone. I wasn't the one behind bars, in a foreign land away from comforts and joyful things, but I was miserable and depressed. Maybe what I needed was Islam, too.

I couldn't fill the void with chess and coffee. I couldn't have a meaningful relationship with any of the other guards aside from Bradley. My relationship with my wife was strained because of the distance and time apart, and my misery and mindset at GTMO made it impossible for me to even feel like calling her. Since I could find no relief talking with her about things at GTMO, our strained conversations became shorter and shorter, and ultimately so meaningless there didn't seem to be much point in even calling her.

Drinking may have been the way some people spent their nights when not at work, but I couldn't think of anything worse than coming to work in that awful place hung-over. I was never really good at sports, having taken little interest in being outside at all. I did what I do best: I hit the books. It made it easier to deal with the monotony and daily struggle of GTMO, and made it easier for me to understand that my marriage was failing. What was left for me that brought any amount of light into my world was my study of the Quran. My intellectual life involved studying the Quran, hadith, the prisoners, the war, and the history behind it all. I found an amazing website called 'Cageprisoners' that would become my tool for learning anything and everything about the prisoners over whom I watched.

Nothing—from the falsely represented military, to the long-distance marriage I had—made sense any more. As I read more about Islam and continued my reading of the Quran, it was beginning to sink in that Islam simply made sense. The Quran was not a confusing book to understand or apply, even to my life. What had seemed at first to be something very foreign and strange gradually became familiar and comfortable.

I took simple steps at first: changing my diet, then eliminating negative music and video games. I found that for each door I was closing for God, God was opening more for me. Changing my diet caused me to feel better and perform better at work. Eliminating the negative music and video games changed my general disposition and attitude and helped me feel more positive, and in touch with the world. As for drinking, no explanation is needed to demonstrate what not drinking does for the body, mind and soul.

Eliminating those unnecessary vices gave me more time to read, more time to learn and more time to reflect on my current situation. I began to spend time in chat rooms with Muslims, asking more questions and getting more answers. I used the chat rooms to further my understanding of the Arabic language. My actions online, as they were in person, were monitored, and both raised eyebrows among my superiors. One day my staff sergeant came knocking unexpectedly at my front door.

"So what is this I hear that you are going to extremist chat rooms on the internet?" SSG Johnsville demanded, without so much as a 'hello'.

"That is crazy, SSG, why would I do that?" I replied.

"I don't know, but look, you are probably going to get arrested for doing that. You know everything we do on the internet is monitored. I cannot help you here, you best just pack your bags and be ready to go," he said to me as he walked away from my front door.

That short, disturbing conversation was enough to deter me from the chat rooms thereafter. It made me feel that there was no one in the world who had an interest in protecting me, or supporting me in gaining knowledge, not even my leadership. Couldn't they see that I was making an effort to 'be-all-I-could-be'? That was obviously not the case, because I was being discouraged. The conflict of interest (in my view) had no relation to my learning Arabic or learning about the prisoners— rather, it lay in the censure of that interest. In my confused state, embroiled between the Army and Islam, I honestly felt that my superiors should support my endeavors to educate myself about Islam. I had forgotten that it was made clear at the beginning of my training that Islam was that which we were at war with.

Islam felt so natural a belief and ideology, presenting something new in the context of my previous readings and religious studies. I had never connected in mind or soul with any of the latter. Rather, I had made jokes and poked fun at people with religious conviction.

Rays of hope for my studies shined through random encounters with the prisoners whom I had cultivated relationships with: Shaker Aamer and Ahmed Errachidi. Aside from them and the Quran, *The Complete Idiot's Guide to Islam* was my constant companion and resource.

My study was quickly becoming less of a distraction from work, and more the ground of my existence, my work becoming the distraction.

One day I woke up, joining the others at the usual morning formation and the mundane discussion of the day's upcoming workload. Usually I knew I was going to be working the block, so I didn't pay much attention to what was being said. My head in the clouds, I was jolted back to earth by hearing my 1st sergeant yelling my name.

"Holdbrooks.....HOLDBROOKS....where the hell is Holdbrooks!?"

"Yes, First Sergeant?" I responded after realizing I was being called on. Running to him, I stood in front of my first sergeant and awaited orders.

"Good news! You're not working the camp today. Go back to sleep and report to the hospital at 1400 hours. You're on special detail."

"Yes, first sergeant." I replied as I took the form from him and ran off back to bed.

I was wondering what this detail was, and why it involved the hospital: there were only a few prisoners there, and the medical staff usually took care of them.

1400 hours came around and I arrived at the hospital, more curious than ever to discover what I would be doing. I was in fact so curious that attempting to go back to sleep had proved to be futile; my interest in the day's work kept me awake. As an

102

MP, I knew I'd be guarding someone. If a prisoner was going to have an operation, then a guard was posted with the prisoner for 12 hours on, 12 hours off, until the prisoner was healed.

I walked in, and saw someone who did not look like a prisoner. The man was in the inpatient room directly next to the nurses' station, an odd place for a recuperating guard to be placed. I looked at the captain who was standing nearby and explained that I was there for the special assignment.

"Aha, so you are going to be with Mr. Hicks for the next two days. Okay, I suppose you can go ahead and make yourself comfortable; he is in the room just outside the office," the captain said. I walked in and realized that the individual I had thought was a guard was a prisoner of GTMO, and not just any prisoner: he was the original prisoner, the one brought to GTMO when it 'opened': David Hicks.

He was asleep, in recovery after an operation. It was required that he be monitored at all times by a guard, so I was to sit for the next two days with him. I addressed him as Mr. Hicks while we conversed over the next two days.

He awoke a few hours after I started my shift, asking what time it was and when he would be able to eat.

"It's about 1630 right now, and you'll be eating at 1700, as usual," I answered. "So, what happened?" Hicks told me about his operation, and how he was surprised that everything went so smoothly. The reason I hadn't ever seen him before was because he was from Camp Echo. He therefore expressed amazement that he was being treated nicely for once. It was easily explained.

In GTMO, soldiers were dealing with the prisoners all day and night, and eventually grew tired and frustrated. On the other hand, the medics and doctors that worked in the hospital didn't have to deal with them daily, nor were they exposed to what took place in the Camp on a day-to-day basis. They were still very professional in their duties, still showing compassion and care for the well-being of the prisoners. To them, the prisoners were not objects or obstacles, but patients.

Hicks was in for a minor operation, nothing too serious. He was, to my delight, open to discussion. He told me his whole story, including how he had discovered Islam. He spoke without hesitation about his youth in Australia and his time in the Taliban. It was amazing to my ears (and quite shocking) hearing this prisoner admitting his guilt and relaying the story of his experiences fighting in Afghanistan. For nearly five months I had been working in GTMO, hearing every single prisoner declaring his innocence, and here was this white Australian explaining his reasons for fighting.

"Some people just don't have anyone to help defend them," Hicks explained. He spoke about his fighting in Albania years earlier, through to the present conflict. He reasoned that it was a moral and religious obligation to go and fight on behalf of the weak and oppressed. Later, he told me of his time in Pakistan and Afghanistan, his conversion to Islam and his travels; he was an open book.

Hicks initially traveled to Albania to fight on the Kosovo side with the belief that he was fulfilling a humane obligation, nothing religious. After leaving Kosovo he began studying Islam, feeling compelled to travel to Pakistan to further his studies.

What struck me as odd was that he was not denying having fought against NATO forces, or having met Osama bin Laden. Given that we stood on opposing sides of the conflict, I was struck by the similarities between us. I felt that Hicks had been beguiled by religious propaganda, where I had been deceived and recruited to fight by political propaganda.

I understood why Hicks had felt motivated to go and fight in Albania, but not in Pakistan. Hicks explained that at first it wasn't for the fighting that he went there. It was education; the fighting followed. Hicks had always wanted to be in the military, so I supposed that he was, in a way, fulfilling his dream. I related to that, having regard for the military's culture of discipline and order, and was attracted to Islam because of these two same things.

My thoughts drifted back to the other prisoners. Unlike Hicks, they had not been captured with guns in their hands.

They all had stories that were perfectly legitimate and reasonable. Some even had proof on government-issued paper that they were not where the Army said they were, or doing what the Army said they were doing. Many reported having been rounded up and sold to U.S. forces overseas. While meeting a guilty prisoner made me feel that perhaps GTMO was not entirely useless or evil, the endless abuses of those who appeared entirely innocent outweighed the benefit of holding one guilty man. It weighed heavily on my conscience, although I could do nothing about it. So I turned again to my books.

From Bad to Worse

Many stories come out of horrible places like GTMO. It would be nice to believe that some of the more disturbing ones are not true. It would also be nice to believe that America does not sanction the use of torture or abuse of its prisoners of war. It would be nice to believe America doesn't tolerate the debasement of prisoners to extract information. However, life (and especially in a place like GTMO) isn't generally nice. In Islam it is understood that difficulties in this life are tests. At GTMO the prisoners were tested greatly.

One such test took place in the JIF buildings. It was the source of a story that later found its way into the mainstream media. I was there when it occurred, but was not myself a witness of the incident. To this day, I question the viability of such an action, and who authorized it. I also wonder who in the American military could come up with such a tactic. I had just escorted a prisoner to interrogation, and had stopped for a smoke afterwards directly outside the JIF building. A fellow MP and I heard three individuals leaving the JIF: two men and a woman.

The men were congratulating her on the skills and tactics she had just employed in interrogation. Out of sheer morbidity, I looked to the other end of the building and watched a prisoner emerge, crying, escorted by Pvt. Enrique. I knew I would hear an account from him later. The prisoner had some blood on his face, which was not unusual as sometimes things got physical in interrogation. I thought perhaps the crying was the result of that roughness. I continued with my day, none the wiser.

It was obvious that I was not the only one at GTMO to see that prayer was what gave the prisoners their strength. Although I was in awe of it, interrogators looked upon that strength as a challenge to their power. A Saudi man, the crying prisoner had reportedly been a student at a flight school in the United States. I learned later what had transpired in that interrogation via a published interview-article with the translator who was present at the time of the interrogation.

The prisoner was seated and shackled to the floor. He was forced to hunch forward, and was told to be cooperative. The female I saw leaving the JIF had reportedly told the prisoner that this was going to be unpleasant for him. After a break, the interrogators returned to the interrogation room. She stood in front of the prisoner, and began unbuttoning her BDU to reveal a tightly fitting t-shirt underneath.

She proceeded to try to sexually entice him. He refused to look at her and kept his gaze fixed on the translator. Other prisoners have reported similar stories of female interrogators using sexual predation to break them. The interrogators reportedly believed that sexual molestation would violate personal and Islamic tenets, dividing a prisoner from Allah. In this case, and at this level of questioning, it evidently wasn't working. In fact, the translator reported in the interview I had read that this type of questioning had never resulted in any intelligence gathered.

Circling around the prisoner, the female put her hand down her pants.

"This is menstrual blood," she reportedly said, then wiped what had come onto her hand on the prisoner's face.

The prisoner, overcome with disgust, then reportedly lunged forward, right out of his shackles. MPs had to come in and bring him back into the chair and re-shackle him.

"Have fun trying to pray tonight when there's no water in your cell to clean up with," the interrogator told the prisoner. The prisoner responded with silence. After that he was taken out of interrogation, at which point I saw him crying.

I asked Enrique later that evening what had occurred. "I don't know, but it was strange. We were told to turn off his water and take away his shower privileges when we returned him to his cell," Enrique reported. The water had stayed off for the following three days. For non-Muslims, having menstrual blood on one's face for that long would be disgusting enough, but Islam encourages the one who prays to be as clean as possible, so it must have been nearly unbearable for that prisoner to function with that blood on his face. In addition, observant Muslim men do not touch women other than their wives, mothers, sisters, or aunts. That act was an attack on several levels of the man's mind and soul, hence his tears upon leaving interrogation.

However they wanted to measure how many days to leave the water off, or just how and by which method to make the prisoners feel unable to pray. Prayer is always accessible for a Muslim, as Islam instructs one on how to purify oneself when water is not available. Whether this fact was known to JIF (or to that prisoner) is irrelevant, because the intention was to break the prisoner—emotionally, mentally and spiritually. In my view it was more in service to abuse for its own sake, rather than for purposes of interrogation. Believing it likely that the prisoner had nothing to tell JIF anyway—that he was innocent—it was overwhelming to consider that the event actually occurred. I made myself believe that what was circulating among my fellow soldiers was true: that it was not in fact blood, but ink.

My faith in the Army was already on shaky ground. I would not entertain the thought that the Bush Administration would allow that to happen at GTMO. I saw later that this was the way they operated, leaving laws vague and undefined so that the individuals that conducted these acts could be as creative, morbid and morally repugnant as they wanted to be. It was all legal in the end, because nothing was written in black and white. Additionally, it all took place on Cuban soil, in a legal limbo between American and Cuban law, a place of no worldly consequences.

The prisoners all reported that it had definitely been blood. I quizzed them, unbelieving.

"How can you be so sure?" I asked them.

"Because you can feel the difference in blood. It is gritty, and it has a smell to it unlike any other," they replied, being no strangers to the texture and smell of their own blood. Regardless of these clear arguments, Bradley and I both refused to accept it, as we discussed the matter over chess. We decided it had to have been ink, and the matter was settled. Unsettled in my heart, I lost sleep over the issue. The ugly truth of the matter was that regardless of whether or not it was blood, the interrogator had made the prisoner think it was indeed her menstrual blood. The prisoners believed it, too. Mission accomplished. However, of what benefit to the mission was that?

Things at GTMO were clearly getting out of hand. What cemented this in my mind was the night I was awoken at 0130 for a PT run by my squad leader. Smelling of beer and cigarette smoke, I didn't know if my squad leader was serious or not. Nonetheless, I followed orders, put on my clothes, and walked outside to a formation of drunken soldiers and leaders alike.

The sober enlisted men were pitifully at the mercy of the Regime members.

"Well, ladies, we decided that things are a little too soft around here, so we are going to PT till it's time to work," said SSG Johnsville. He was clearly drunk, and as the bickering between him and Sgt. Parks continued throughout the PT run, it became clear that this was all the result of a drunken dispute between them. They expected this PT exercise to prove whose men were better, stronger and hated the prisoners more. It was what we called a 'pissing match' between the two. The rest of the Regime wanted to join in, and see who actually had the 'better' soldiers.

So we started running. We ran all the mountain trails, covering a good fifteen miles of terrain that night, stopping only for one of the Regime members to vomit.

"1, 2, 3, going to do PT, then go to work, and slam a detainee," Sgt. Parks was singing as he ran. Those that refused to sing with him were made to do sprints in circles until everyone was singing louder.

"We're going to see who is strong, we're going to see who is right, we're going to see who is tough, we're going to do PT all night," Johnsville sang after him. This continued for nearly two hours. We stopped and did sprints or grass drills (various aerobic exercises), and ran some more, following our drunken leaders into the night.

"Osama bin Laden is a stupid-a** f***, hiding in the caves like a lame a** duck, we're gonna beat Al-Qaeda and the Taliban too, and then go home and kill us some Jews," sang Sgt. Parks.

I thought with that last song I'd heard the worst of it, only for it to be topped by more abusive language as the night dragged on. They had deprived their fellow soldiers of sleep, used racist epithets and conducted PT drunk. The first sergeant, who started to ask around after it was all over, noticed something was amiss.

"How did you sleep last night?" he would ask us at random, "So you were just doing a standard PT program, right?" He was hoping one of us would slip and expose the Regime—which he already knew about—but that he had been unable to track down. The soldiers all knew better than to take the bait. We were more afraid of the Regime than the expectations of our supervising officer. We answered the queries with answers that were best for the Regime.

I, along with undoubtedly every other soldier, thought *I'm not going to be the one to slip and say that there was something going on, and first sergeant wasn't in control.* If I uttered a word against the Regime, I would have guaranteed that my check was cashed: life would be more of a hell for me than it already was.

We all performed poorly that day, and the first sergeant duly noted it. Since no one would slip and talk about what happened, he decided that he would lead PT after work that same day. He did exactly the same route and exercises as the drunken run the previous night, without the racial slurs and alcohol. He ran us till everyone was dehydrated or vomiting, or both. Still we kept our silence. It infuriated him that he was not the one in control, that we were loyal to someone else and would not obey him. He kept a much closer eye on us, but there were too many people for him to watch. The real control of the unit was in their hands, but the first sergeant could do little else but fuss and fume about it.

The abused soldiers unwittingly supported the Regime. Thus encouraged, the Regime members merrily continued their transgressions. They appeared to love the trouble they caused, and now at least two ERF teams were kept on standby. These two teams were largely voluntary, which benefited me as I tried to avoid having to participate in ERFs. By not volunteering, I was left to do my regular duties.

One cool October afternoon as I arrived at work, I was greeted at the sally-port doors by four officers and six other officials from the medical field. Every afternoon that October, like clockwork, there were rainstorms that would blow in for a few hours, cooling things off for the night. On that day, even the weather wasn't sufficient to cool things off.

They were standing in front of a large medical case depicting a red cross, discussing something. I spotted Bradley at the end of the meeting area, leaning against the cleaning supply closet, and asked him what was going on.

"I didn't ask, all I heard was they're waiting for somebody from medical to show up and debrief everyone about some health threat or something," Bradley replied. My curiosity was naturally piqued when something out of the norm occurred on base, and when it did, first sergeant told us before work.

One of the medical personnel came forward and addressed us.

"There is a potential health threat that needs to be taken care of today, soldiers. It should go smoothly; standby for your briefing," he said. I knew there had been a few prisoners with TB and that everyone had been tested, but what kind of health threat could there be? Three people from medical were cleared into Camp 4 and approached the case with the red cross.

Standing toward the back with Bradley, I leaned against the cleaning closet and listened. Two male medics stood in front of a pretty blonde nurse who opened the medical case.

"It's time to administer flu shots for the year, everyone. There shouldn't be any issues, but you will all have a role here. Some of you will be opening the bean holes, others holding detainee's arms, and others helping with the trash and what have you," said the nurse. We were then split up into different groups with our different jobs. I would be holding the prisoners' arms as they got their flu shot, which I considered to be very boring. I wondered to myself: *What a joke, if it's just a flu shot, why all the commotion?*

We started in Camp 4. The first block of prisoners went smoothly, as did the second. A few prisoners raised questions such as: 'What is this shot?', 'Why shot?', 'No shot, you're going to kill us!', but as soon as they were done ranting a translator would explain things, returning calm and order again. Twenty minutes into the job, we started on the third block, so for all intents and purposes we would be done and it would be over shortly.

An older prisoner came forward for his shot. I felt a quiver in his arm as the needle entered, and a little bit of blood trickled out as the needle exited. The prisoner then fell to the ground, nearly pulling me through the bean hole. That is when all hell broke loose.

"DON'T GET THE SHOT, THEY ARE GOING TO KILL US!!" the prisoners started to yell, and everything exploded into an uproar in the seconds that followed. The elderly prisoner had merely fainted at the sight of his own blood. I noted that this fear of blood could not possibly exemplify the 'worst-of-the-worst'. All the prisoners yelled and screamed, spat on the guards and kicked the mesh. Not one of them would cooperate, and as they began yelling louder and louder; it reached the point that the translators could not even talk to them.

Within seconds, word had spread to all the prisoners in Camp Delta that they were going to be killed through this medical procedure. Again, the efficiency of their communication amazed me. To restore order, we had to call in an ERF crew to Camp 4, which I hadn't seen before then.

Those prisoners willing to cooperate went back into their common areas, and those who were still refusing to work with the guards were OC sprayed and then detained. They were shackled, received the shot, and left to cool off. There were ten prisoners left in the common area, but none made any attempts against the guards. If they were going to get at the guards, it would have been a perfect time to exact some revenge, but nothing happened. For the rest of the hour, we gave the remaining fifteen prisoners their shots. What should have taken us twenty-five minutes to do instead required an hour, and that was only for Camp 4.

In the meantime, pandemonium had ensued in Camps 1, 2, and 3. As efficient as their communication system was, the prisoners were so confused that many had heard stories that the guards were systematically executing the prisoners in Camp 4, and stories that the flu shot was in fact anthrax.

Every single prisoner was fighting with the guards in Camp 1. After trying to calm them and get them to comply, we eventually had to use ERF. Additional soldiers were called in to form ERF teams and they were told to bring extra clothing, because all the prisoners had to arm themselves was their own bodily waste, hurled from cups.

"You cannot kill us, this is not right! The world will know of what you have done here today!" they were yelling, along with an assault of other phrases in Arabic. Four hours into the shift, only two more blocks of prisoners had been given their shots. Nearly every prisoner got an ERF. The manpower was just not there for this scale of operation due to the panic that had arisen in the camps. Guards were becoming tired or, as in the case of Sgt. Parks, overly excited. He was running into cells screaming things like 'Yee-haw', and 'Here we come, rag-head!' each time he went in to subdue a panicked prisoner.

Volunteering for ERF after ERF, Parks incited the first sergeant who witnessed his intense hatred and anger. It wasn't helpful at all to the situation that the rest of the Regime members were telling the prisoners things like, "Oh, you're going to get yours now: time to meet your maker." The sight of Parks struck fear in me, so I couldn't imagine how it felt to be his prisoner. Then there was SSG Johnsville, cheering on the increasingly aggressive guards, adding fuel to the already-blazing fire. Another unit was called in to work with us. We went through more cans of OC spray that single day than any other period of time throughout the entire year I was there.

Prisoners were getting kicked and slammed, and punched right and left. Some, out of fear, broke off the faucets to their sinks and fashioned them into knives, hoping perhaps the guards would not enter their cells. Some of them successfully punctured the necks of some of the guards, but there were no serious injuries received. I was eventually relieved for a moment to take a smoke break. I ran. I ran as fast as I could to the smoking area and sat there, trying to understand what was going on. It was too much to take in, like being in the thick of a war without guns; it felt so strange, and wrong.

After his fifty-third ERF, Parks was finally pulled off the ERF detail by the first sergeant, as the other units started showing up to help out. I managed to maneuver back in as if I had been there the whole time despite having escaped the block for nearly an hour. As Sgt. Parks was pulled off, Smitty took his place. After two or three ERF's, he was so high with anger and excitement that when I looked him in the eyes, I saw no one there.

"What makes the green grass grow? BLOOD, BLOOD, BRIGHT RED BLOOD!" he would scream as he went charging in, "We're going to turn GTMO green you sand niggers!"

It was SSG Johnsville who tutored all of them in abusing power. The official manual on manipulating people, abusing prisoners and getting promoted for it was licensed and copy-written by Johnsville. Smitty was a devoted disciple, and together with their pals from the Regime, they represented everything corrupt and illegitimate about GTMO Bay.

I was horrified. I couldn't help but think to myself: *How embarrassing that these are my fellow soldiers*. Other soldiers had to be pulled off and assigned to lower-stress jobs on base. However, there were always volunteers available for Extreme Reaction Force. It was a disgrace. I had worked hard with the prisoners, trying to show that some guards actually thought and had compassion, only to have it trampled upon. It made me want to be anywhere but there. It dragged on. What should have been a simple eight-hour shift turned into an entire community effort that went on for nearly twenty-three hours!

Upon entering Camp 3, I was glad to see a familiar face, Shaker Aamer. I explained the situation to Aamer, and asked his help in calming everyone. He looked very critically into my eyes for a moment, and then spoke to the prisoners in the block. After that, only a few prisoners were still fighting with us. Moving on to another block, I saw Ahmed Errachidi.

Errachidi asked me what was going on. In a tired and worn voice, I gave a summary of events.

"A prisoner fainted in Camp 4 when we started this nearly seventeen hours ago, and everyone thinks we are trying to kill you all, despite the fact that no one has died. This is just crazy, please help me!"

Errachidi spoke to the surrounding prisoners in Arabic and they all calmed down. The prisoners in the whole block relaxed and were complacent. My team leader, Sgt. Green, duly noted this sudden change in the atmosphere. Through the rest of the night, we fought and struggled to give the rest of the prisoners their flu shots. There were so many accounts of prisoners acting out and deserving of reprimand that it was deemed to be pointless to take any further disciplinary action. We simply couldn't process all the work and information we had received in that shift. In the end, it was a nightmare.

Twenty-three hours after having begun what might have been a simple task, it was over and I was headed home. I was so relieved to be away from the camp. The next day I awoke and was greeted by Sgt. Green. He wanted to know what I had said that calmed those two blocks, and why I was able to do it. I explained that I had developed a great working relationship with those two prisoners, and that they would listen to me. I further explained that those two men in particular exhibited great control on their respective blocks. Green thanked me for my help, and spoke not one more word to me about it.

I was expecting that he would congratulate me for my tact in securing a relationship with such influential prisoners, or even be grateful to the two prisoners for their help. I saw after my explanation, however, that Errachidi and Aamer were switched from block to block and sent to interrogation more often than before, even leaving the camp altogether. What I had

116

said had quickly spurred the interest of the JIF, which wasn't my intention. It depressed me that even when I wanted to do something good—like try to explain that not all the prisoners were evil—it was still twisted into something bad, and added to the suffering of those behind bars. After my inadvertent contribution to the JIF, those two prisoners never again had a life at GTMO that you might call normal.

Any semblance of normality in the camp was deleted. There was high tension between the prisoners and the guards in the days that followed. A blessing of the experience was that I was now known as the nice guard, and so had more requests for conversation than anyone else on duty. For days, the prisoners wouldn't talk, or stop talking, depending on the prisoner.

That night of horrors started what was the longest hunger strike that I witnessed while I was in GTMO; some prisoners didn't eat for 39 days straight. Eventually they started dropping like flies from malnutrition, dehydration and other health issues. The hospital was packed, and the prisoners were not giving up.

It seemed silly, at first. The prisoners were making themselves only more miserable in a place that was already designed to achieve that. I suspected that the guards took pleasure in their self-inflicted hunger pain. As time went on, I saw that it was all they had, and they were clever about it; even if the guards didn't care, the higher-ups would, especially if any prisoners died in the process. Dead prisoners are not good for morale.

The corpsmen were angry with the guards for the situation, and they were in turn angry with the prisoners, who were striking in the first place as an expression of anger towards the guards. Their only substantial counter, the prisoners had little else with which to express themselves. At the time, I didn't understand the religious implications, but fasting is one way for a Muslim to keep himself in check, to suppress his base desires, and grow closer to Allah. Giving up food and drink insulted the Army, but reminded the prisoners to be grateful and to seek out the blessings of Allah. The blessings of Allah are everywhere, even in GTMO. The prisoners also thought that fasting might

117

get the attention of someone important (with an ounce of conscience) to make a decision to change things, which did happen, to a small degree.

I knew the Army and its people well, and understood soon after my arrival that mercy and compassion did not exist except among the prisoners, for one other. It was something that I felt would be to no avail, and I respected those on hunger strikes enough to tell them so. They made the decision to make this hellhole even more hellish by denying themselves food and drink in protest of their being caged unjustly. I did not understand why or for what reasons they could possibly want to do this to themselves, but they were obviously very driven. While my fellow guards simply noted that the food trays had been taken back without being touched, I took note instead of how many days each prisoner had refused his food. As some of the prisoners continued ignoring their food trays, I began to worry about them. The Cuban heat was hard enough to endure without dehydration.

Eventually command had to step in and take some initiative. Linguists appeared on the block and tried to reason with the prisoners. Privileges were given to those who broke their fast, as an inspiration to eat. I began to worry more about Errachidi, and the resolve with which they fasted inspired me to a deeper interest in Islam.

Either With or Against Us

When one is being bullied, the thought often arises: *Why can't these people just leave me alone?* One of life's great mysteries is why bullies must relentlessly abuse those under them. One wonders why they have nothing else they'd rather do with their time. A lot of time and energy goes into the act of bullying. Schoolyard and cyber-bullies torment and aggravate, but bullying often subsides due to boredom, intervention, or the victim removing themselves from the environment. The bullying of which I fell victim had a certain aim that was determined, could not be contravened and afforded me little chance of escape.

I simply could not suppress my naturally inquisitive nature. That was my weakness. Talking with the prisoners—who were more interesting and more knowledgeable about the war and the world than my fellow soldiers—was getting me into trouble.

It began by shifting all duties to me when I was at work. Their aim was to make me as busy as possible so that I had no time to converse with the prisoners. I would respond to the challenge by working faster and harder so that I could still speak with them. The more time I was witnessed talking with prisoners, the more some of the guards (mostly those of the Regime) began harassing me and watching my every move.

To them, speaking with the prisoners meant nothing else than treachery. With watchful eyes, they waited to see whether my conversations with the prisoners would translate into action of some sort, such as sabotage or the leaking of information. Nightly binge-drinking and hatred clouded their thinking. They could not understand why I would rather talk with the prisoners, even though their conversations never varied from the core subjects of sports, women, or hate-mongering. Their conversations were about as enlightened as the inside of a lizard's hole.

Observing that my work was done efficiently, the authorities decided to limit my shifts to when the prisoners were asleep. I also got the jobs on swing shift that had me working the sally-port or prisoner escorts, which were the two toughest jobs in which to converse with prisoners. Yet I found ways and other opportunities to continue my thirst for knowledge.

The verbal altercations with my fellow soldiers were simple to brush off, as I have never cared for other people's opinions of me. In my mind, when other soldiers or my superiors would make an off comment, I would reply inwardly *'whatever'*, although outwardly I would give a false impression of concern.

The physical altercations, if they had come from my peers, would have been nearly as easy to overlook and explain away as the verbal, but the blows dealt to me came from the hands, feet and knees of my superiors. Being beaten up by peers for being different would have been reminiscent of high school, but I was not used to those above me resorting to this behavior. *What did it matter,* I thought to myself, *if I speak to the prisoners and learn from them, while doing my duties and job well?*

Logic and clarity of mind did not factor into the Regime's thinking. They clearly ran the company. Between this abuse and the fraternization that was taking place on a daily basis, it was clear to me that the Regime was both out of control and unstoppable.

As I grew more and more comfortable speaking with the prisoners, I grew less and less concerned about being witnessed or overheard by others. I did not see any point in trying to convince my superiors that I was merely passing the time or improving my efficiency. I was finding joy—for the first time since I arrived—in those precious conversations, and I didn't care who knew it. My disregard of their opinions produced more rage from the Regime members, a taste of which I experienced one evening after work.

I sat in my house, trying to find something on the eleven TV channels made available. Channel surfing, I heard SSG Johnsville knock at my door. I answered and looked at him, noting alcohol on his breath.

"What is going on, Sergeant? You need me for something?" I asked.

"Yeah, Holdbrooks, I am going to need you to come on over by my place for a bit. We need to iron some things out," he drawled.

Having already been to the squad leader's home a few times before, I didn't think much of the request at the time. We walked in and, oddly, there wasn't anyone else around. Johnsville went out back, and I followed. As I exited the door to the backyard, I found the Regime in all its glory, sitting there drinking beers, Copenhagen in their mouths, with Marlboros at their sides. I was asked to close the door, which I did. I saw instantly that this was going to be less an intervention and more of a good ol' boy stomping session.

"Holdbrooks, we asked you to come out here today because of some serious issues that seem to be arising all around you," Johnsonville started. "We have a little concern. You see Holdbrooks, we feel that you want to be with those pieces of sh** we are serving each day, and if that is the case, we can arrange it for you." Before I got a chance to answer, another question was posed.

"What is going through your mind when you are in the camp, Holdbrooks?" SSG Woods inquired, pointing at me using the hand with which he held his beer. I offered my prepared and often-repeated answer.

"Well, I am thinking about how I can get the job done, how to make the day easy, and how to get out of here with the best mood I can have when I leave work," I replied. Rather than pacify them, my response heightened the tension.

"That is bullsh**; you want to be their friends! I see you talking to them, becoming their friends, asking them about Islam...you want to be a Muslim, is that it?" Sgt. Parks exclaimed, taking a step towards me. At this point I knew that a pounding was imminent. I then thought I might as well try, since I had their attention, to express my views.

"No Sergeant. I am simply learning what I can. This is a great chance for all of us to learn what life is like from people all around the world, from different countries, faiths and educations, and I just feel we should take advantage of that." My words couldn't have fallen on more deaf ears. To the corn-fed minds of the Regime, this was an insult to their way of life, their being 'American'. It angered them further to suggest they could learn anything more than what they already knew, let alone from those they guarded. Drawing nearer to me, they began circling me like pack dogs.

"You listen to me Holdbrooks; I will beat the Taliban out of you. They are not people. They are detainees. You are not supposed to be talking to them; it says that in our SOP. You want to go and be a traitor to America, then I have no problem kicking the living sh** out of you right now," SSG Burns threatened. That wasn't their actual, personal problem with me. It was Sgt. Parks who came out with their real issues.

"What exactly is your deal here? What is your problem Holdbrooks? Why can't you just go to work, get the job done, keep your mouth shut, and get off of work and have a beer like the rest of us? You don't need to feel anything for these detainees; you don't need to care about them. They will die here. What is your problem, Holdbrooks?" As they fumed, they added more imaginative threats.

"You need to get your head on straight. Sympathy is the sign of a traitor."

"We could just lock you up with the rest of the detainees if you like them so much."

"I am going to skull f*** the Taliban out of you."

"Don't make me skull drag you through the camp and let those detainees know who is really in charge."

The Army is not a wise forum to voice individual opinions, as it is threatened by intelligence and thrives on indifference. It is historically proven that those with an opposing stance are the recipients of bullying and abuse, merely because of their originality and uniqueness. It was insulting to these all-American boys not only that I was not like them, but that I didn't want to be like them. The fact that I did not square with the idea that it was bad to speak to the prisoners, treachery to respect them in any way, and un-American to not hate them only infuriated those in the Regime, and they took that anger out on me that evening.

It all came to a head when Sgt. Parks got about an inch from my face and threatened me.

"Why don't you hate these dirt bags, they're nothing but a bunch of American-hating terrorists and you know that. If you don't give me one damn good reason why you don't hate them then I am going to get medieval on your a**, Private."

At this point the futility of avoiding violence was clear, so I replied with an answer that I knew would not change their mood: "Because that is not my disposition."

The next thing I remembered was that I was picking myself up and swinging back as hard as I could at Parks. Then the others joined the party. I may have been able to hold my own against one or perhaps two, but the whole Regime were on me. Through their alcohol-induced fog, they forgot all the rules of protocol. Discipline was not to be meted out in this manner. There was a verbal advisory, then a written letter. Physically abusing your subordinates was a serious breach of protocol.

Eventually, after a few more blows were exchanged, SSG Johnsville must have realized that he had stepped out of line. They all had. It could lead to serious trouble for hitting someone of such a lower rank, someone for whom they were responsible and, more importantly, someone for whose safety they were responsible.

Johnsville stepped in to break it up, but not without a final warning to me.

"You best get your head on straight. Now go home, and don't you think about mentioning this to anyone, or your life will be hell for the rest of the time we are here. You understand, Private?" he growled into my face. I didn't dignify him with an answer. I lit up a cigarette, walked through the house and let the door bang shut after me. As I walked out the door, I asked myself if this was brought about because of what occurred on flu-shot day—my talking with the prisoners. I allowed myself other questions. *Did I somehow bring this on myself? Was my curiosity out of place, or out of control?*

The mixture of the taste of blood and smoke in my mouth—adrenaline pumping through my veins—ended the argument in the negative. I was not always going to be at GTMO; my leaders would be different one day and my fellow soldiers would be replaced by others. Life would continue for me, and I was not going to behave in a way that I would regret years later. Oddly enough, the encounter was just what I needed to confirm that how I was conducting myself was well and good. I didn't care to stoop down to their level to please those in the Regime, who were less open-minded and less intelligent. It was clear from their continued hostility that I intimidated them. I was not hated by the prisoners like they were; I better understood the world they came from, and the world we were in. To agree to their wishes was to conform, and I never had been a conformist. That evening was as bad as it got, although I saw it coming. They never entirely left me alone, before or after that evening. I already understood from other verbal and physical abuses that they hated me, and hated what I was trying to do. They just used that evening as an opportunity to let off more steam than usual.

Later, I considered what exactly I could do about it. I couldn't go directly to the first sergeant or the commander, as that would be skipping rank. The one to whom I would report this was the one who had himself committed the abuse. On the other hand, while they were totally out of line breaching protocol, so was I in talking openly with the prisoners. Any report about it would result in me drawing undue attention to myself, and I wanted to continue conducting myself in this way as long as I possibly could.

I decided I didn't care enough about what happened at the 'meeting' at SSG Johnsville's place to cause any fuss about it, as it would generally be counter-productive. I let it slide.

The silver lining of it all took place in the morning. In the company of the Regime members, the first sergeant asked me what had happened to my face. I glanced at the Regime members, noting the fear on their faces. Looking back at my first sergeant, I answered:

"I missed a softball. It hit me square in the face."

"Do you think I'm dumb, Private?" he asked me.

"No, Sir. It was a softball, First Sergeant, that's all." I repeated.

The air was still for a moment as the Regime members held their collective breath. The first sergeant dropped the matter. His closing remark on the issue was as rewarding as a medal for me, and made up for the night before.

"If you have the intestinal fortitude to keep to yourself what happened, then you have heart. You're more of a soldier than whoever hit you."

Thus affirmed, I acknowledged to myself that I had won the first battle against the Regime.

Whatever power they felt they held over the camps was now limited. For all their fussing and fighting, they had no power over me, and now they knew it.

Muslim MP

It dawned on me at long last. The guys in the Regime needed their booze and each other to feel validated in their behavior. I, on the other hand, felt at home with the prisoners, so awed by their resilience and peace with their horrible circumstances...and yet for myself, I felt no real inner peace. I enjoyed speaking with the prisoners, and yet when I went away from them, going about my routines and duties, I felt an emotional and spiritual vacuum. I could not deny it any longer, although throughout my life I had ridiculed the importance placed on religious beliefs and practices; the truth was I needed religion.

The more I learned about Islam, the more accepting of it I felt. It was neither the words nor the actions of the prisoners that pressured me: the impulse to accept Islam came from within my own heart. The answer to the question I kept asking myself was clear now; it was the reason I was in GTMO. My need for guidance was almost palpable. All my struggling and suffering had to have been occurring for some reason. Deep down, I always believed that.

Proof presented itself over and again that feeling good externally was no key to lasting happiness. I wanted to honestly feel good and whole in myself. I had been reading the Quran virtually since my arrival at GTMO, and I had picked up some hadith from Chaplain Yee. The one time I was able to talk to him about Islam, he actually gave me a wonderful set of books that relayed information about all kinds of matters. I hadn't seen it through all my studying and conversations, but did now: I wanted—no—needed to accept Islam. Allah had shown me the way, but I had previously been distracted and blind.

I had already been implementing bits of Islamic practice into my life. With each change, life for me got better; for every door that I closed, more doors opened. My head was clearer, my time was being spent in more valuable ways, and my overall mental disposition was much more positive. My own implementation of the slightest changes (and observing the prisoners' character and dignity) had proven to me that being a Muslim was what I needed. I was on a mission.

I set out to find Ahmed Errachidi. I wanted to talk to him and embrace Islam in his presence. I could see it in my head, and I knew it was right.

It took me a week to finally find the block that held Errachidi. I wasn't working that block, but went there anyway, walking right past the block sergeant and the guards to begin a conversation with Errachidi. I walked up to him and addressed him with my urgent question.

"Hey, I think I want to become a Muslim. Can you help me? How do I become a Muslim?"

Looking up at me, Errachidi simply replied, "No."

Nothing else followed from Errachidi, except a simple waving of his hand to shoo me away before I spoke any further or protested any longer. His response could have been due to any number of reasons so, feeling puzzled, I walked away.

I went back to the block on which I was supposed to be working, wondering why Errachidi did not seem happy or excited about it, and why he had simply said 'no'. There were certainly others I could have asked to assist me in my acceptance of Islam, but none had taught me nearly as much as Errachidi. I wanted to accept Islam in his presence. Undeterred by this letdown, I didn't give up.

Another week passed. My determination to become a Muslim was unwavering. I felt an intense conviction in my heart; my only confusion about it came from wondering why Errachidi had refused to hear me that day.

I was then switched to night shift again and was sent over to Camp 2 where Errachidi was usually held. On December 23rd, 2003, I began work on the night shift. I was walking down the block, cleaning (as was my duty) and distributing to prisoners soap and brushes with which to clean their cells, when I saw Errachidi again. I instantly stopped what I was doing, looked at him, and squat close to the ground outside his cell. I again told him that I wanted to be a Muslim.

This time, Errachidi took notice of me.

"Why do you want to be a Muslim?" he asked.

A flood of answers poured out of my mouth, everything I'd been thinking, all the things I'd realized I needed in Islam. Many of them in fact had nothing to do with Islam, or being a good Muslim in the slightest, but were all rather trivial as I would find out. Ahmed asked me nicely to shut up, and sit down.

"Listen, Brother," Errachidi interrupted. I stopped in mid-sentence, shocked at being addressed as a brother for the first time.

What followed was a very intense and lengthy conversation between us that lasted for some hours. Errachidi held a precious treasure in his hands, and he wanted to make it clear that no one could share in it unless he had a worthy intention and a commitment to keep the treasure safe. His jealous guarding of the religion just made me more zealous to accept it.

Errachidi spoke of how my family and my life would change, how my fellow soldiers would look at me differently, what would change between me and my wife, and how my friends—no, America itself—would view me if I accepted Islam. He explained what I would and would not be able to do any longer, the commitment that was involved, the discipline and the structure.

"Listen, Brother, do you understand all of the things that will change in your life if you do this? You will not be allowed to drink anymore, to smoke anymore, to eat pork anymore, to have sex outside of marriage, or to look at porn. You will need to learn Arabic. You will need to pray five times a day. You will need to learn this religion, and it will be the governing factor in your life if you really submit yourself to the will of Allah. Your unit is going to look at you differently. You may end up in a cell with us. Your family will look at you differently. Your friends will look at you differently, and your life will become much harder."

He discussed prayer and charity, and observance of the fast of Ramadan. For nearly three hours we covered all these topics and more, and then Errachidi appeared satisfied.

"If you are sure you want to do this, I will tell you how to say the Shahaadah and you will be a Muslim, but there is no turning back after this. Once you have accepted Allah in your heart, and submitted to His Will, you will surely be condemned if you abandon Him. Do you understand?"

I said "yes" and gave Errachidi an index card that I had in my pocket, along with a pen. Errachidi wrote down a transliteration of the Shahaadah for me, and awoke the prisoner next to him. After a brief explanation to the other prisoner (who was initially irritated at being woken up), an excited and willing response followed.

"Ash-hadu an laa ilaaha il Allah, wa ash-hadu anna Muhammadan rasool-Allah (I testify that there is no deity worship but Allah and I testify that Muhammad is the Messenger of Allah)" I read aloud, in a calm and collected tone. The prisoner, acting as witness, congratulated me.

"Allahu Akbar (Allah is the Greatest)", he said, "SubhanAllah (Glory be to Allah)". Both the witness and Errachidi attempted to shake my hand through the wire mesh. He gave me praise, and shared his hopes with me, as Errachidi did. Then Errachidi and I continued talking for a good number of hours afterwards, until three in the morning, at which point he stopped me so he could get some sleep.

"I don't know how many times I will be moved tomorrow; please my brother, let me get some sleep," Errachidi said to me. I thanked him once more and continued my night's work, feeling infinitely better as I wasn't alone anymore. I felt I had finally made that great accomplishment in my life and that I was finally on the right path. It was amazing.

I went home that night and made a clumsy Fajr prayer before heading to sleep. The next night I went to work, walking by the cells of the brothers I would often talk with, and instead of the regular 'Hello', or 'How are you today?', I said "Asalaamu Alaikum," to which they responded with confused looks. It was only a matter of days before they began responding in kind to my Islamic greeting, and within a few more days they initiated the greeting upon sight of me.

News spread quickly among the other prisoners of my conversion—they were excited. Some of those who had never before spoken a word to me (that I had assumed was because of the language barrier) were now praising me in English and welcoming me into the faith. They were all very happy. Work went from being the worst part of my day to the best part, as the prisoners were all friendly and hopeful for me.

To my fellow guards, however, I said nothing. There was no reason to, and every reason not to. I would slip off the end of the block to pray, praying when the prisoners did, and each time they were very surprised to see me observing prayer. It was not lost on the prisoners that I had an even harder time than they practicing Islam in such a place. As for myself, I welcomed the challenge as I felt that with each prayer I was working towards a better life.

My outlook on the world was different. I saw my past mistakes, decisions and trials as trivial, and was amused at how all of it had seemed so grim. The newfound peace in my heart alleviated worries about my wife, my deployment, and the actions of the Regime. I didn't care about the results of what would occur, as the faith in my heart showed me that Allah had a plan for me. If it meant living and working in GTMO for me to find Islam, it was all worth it. Islam made such clear and perfect sense to me so I felt like I had, in this armpit of the world, come home. I felt that even the blood that ran through my veins somehow had new purpose.

I had been lost, drifting from place to place, but now I knew what to do, and I had a path on which to travel. My questions took another turn and intention now: to increase my knowledge about Islam, and to grow in that inner peace and clarity. My questions were now answered about my purpose in life and whether or not Islam was the answer for me. I intensified my studies and research.

Surely Bradley saw it coming, but did not seem to care that I had accepted Islam. He was indifferent, yet to this day I hope that he will find Islam, too. Then I told my roommate.

"As long as you don't get any of us hurt and you keep doing your job well, I don't care what you believe in," my roommate told me, "Wanna go play some soccer?"

The disinterest with which Bradley and my roommate responded to the news of my conversion didn't bother me at all, as I wasn't looking for their support. I was relieved to let them know, so that I could pray around them without hiding. The issues that arose at work, however, did add stress to my life.

Now that it was common knowledge among the prisoners that I was a Muslim too, I got mixed reactions from the prisoners. Some of them would ask me for special privileges, and get upset with me if I could not comply. Others would simply ignore me, and still others would exhibit hostility towards me, accusing me of being a tool for the U.S. Army. There wasn't much that I could do, so I continued my respectful orientation, hoping that I wouldn't be judged. I wanted to be accepted, but I realized that in the high-stress environment they were in, it was inevitable that some of the brothers would be suspicious of me. The methods by which the U.S. Army gathered intelligence were on the minds of all the prisoners on a daily basis. They had stooped to unbelievable levels of immorality to get the answers they wanted, so God knows they were not beyond sending in a spy.

As far as the guards were concerned, now that I was a brother in faith with the prisoners, my sympathy was deepened and my sensitivity towards injustices was more acute. I began to simply disregard certain instructions that we were given to me if they didn't seem equitable, or conducive to efficiency. Non-compliance is a big issue when you are in the military, and I had a minor conflict inside myself about it.

Allah, in His amazing plan, prevented all those that would behave the worst for it from knowing of my conversion. If they did know, I believe Allah prevented them from confronting me on the issue. Of course, after the verbal and physical abuse of which I had been victim, it was clear that those in the Regime saw me as a traitor for showing respect to the prisoners. Although I was already denigrated for my interest in the prisoners and in Islam, it wasn't clear to any of them that I had actually accepted the faith. None of them knew, except for one.

One night after work as I went out back to have some coffee and reflect, Pvt. Michael approached me. He walked up to me from the side.

"Are you okay? You need someone to talk to?" Pvt. Michael said in an antagonizing manner. In a bit of a daze because of the stress of practicing my newfound faith at such a job, I responded, not picking up on the sarcasm in Pvt. Michael's voice.

"You know, sometimes I want to go and see the doctors to see if all the stress I have here is natural, or if I am making 'much ado about nothing'. Sometimes I wish there was an SOP to show us what we are supposed to be doing. It just seems wrong to me sometimes how we treat the detainees, after all, they are people like you and me: they bleed red, you know?" Out of nowhere, Pvt. Michael clocked me on the head and stood over me, glaring at me in anger.

"Mother f***er, if there were an SOP all it would be is trouble. You think Johnsville or Parks is going to hand you a f***ing manual? Where do you think you are? This is where we keep our shame, boy! This is where we do what's needed to keep America safe, and my three kids at home safe, damn it! So don't tell me you've got a problem and you need to see a psychiatrist, man. Don't complain to me if I rat you out: you ratted yourself out, sympathizing with everyone here, and praying outside by the generator every time that nonsense blares over the loudspeaker! You ratted yourself out man, so don't come crying to me and don't ask me for a damn thing anymore. In fact, don't speak to me unless it's absolutely necessary Private, are we clear?"

"I expected it from Smitty or Parks man, but I'd have thought you knew a thing or two about oppression, bro" I responded back. It then dawned on me that Pvt. Michael could have exposed me to the Regime—he had seen me praying. "I thought you'd at least not rat me out to those rednecks—they'd have some choice words for you in civilian life. But I guess I was wrong about that."

"Yeah, you were wrong," he replied. "This isn't about race; this isn't even about religion. This is about who's with the agenda and who's with the enemy, Private Traitor. Now get your a** back up, and don't breathe a word of this to anyone or I'll be giving you more than a sucker punch next time, b****." He turned on his heel and stomped away from me, leaving me to mull over the weight of the exchange.

I felt horrible, betrayed. Pvt. Michael and I had been roommates together for a time, and he'd sold me out to the Regime. It was another lesson learned in GTMO. I didn't have much time to sit and stew about the consequences of the Regime members knowing I prayed like the prisoners, as it was time for me to pack for a trip back home.

The Army had granted me leave, and it couldn't have come at a better time. I was leaving the camp for a quick visit to Arizona. Excited at the prospect that being on Arizona soil would have a calming and balancing effect on me, I began to actually smile.

Before I could get too hopeful, my team leader, Sgt. Green, asked me to meet him in the Regime's house. He told me he would no longer be my team leader, and that Sgt. Parks would be replacing him. Parks then made it clear to me right afterward that he was going to make my life a living hell.

"Enjoy your time away, you f***ing traitor, when you get back I am going to put some America in your a**! I am going to fix you and make you into a real soldier and you will hate all these sand-niggers like you should've all along," he menaced.

"Sergeant, I do not know what you want to hear from me, but you're wrong in your opinion of me. I am not a sympathizer, nor do I want to be like the detainees," I said in response. Then Sgt. Parks punched me right in the face. The conversation was obviously over so I walked away, back to my house and began packing my bag.

Parks was a corn fed, overweight drunkard, if there ever was one. Nearly 32 years of age—and at 5' 10" and about

134

275lbs—he was balding and hygienically repulsive in every manner. Most people are promoted to sergeant within the first three years of their enlistment, but not Parks. It took him longer. When he wasn't eating he either had a bottle of brew or a wad of Copenhagen in his mouth and an empty bottle for spit. Sometimes he had both. Occasionally he would get too drunk to know which bottle was which, and drink from his spit bottle, or spit in his drink bottle. His body odor was perpetually conspicuous, as though he hadn't showered in a week; equally visible were the stains on his BDUs. It was astonishing that such a disreputable creature was promoted to sergeant at all.

External appearances aside, what lay beneath was more disturbing, making me only more fearful. This man thrived on the Bush Administration's propaganda, and was easy prey for the hype the Army was feeding him. Further, Parks had no sympathy or concern for adhering to SOP regarding camp operations, or concerning the prisoners, for that matter. It wouldn't matter if it was, for example, a young and English-speaking Canadian prisoner who had been accused of killing an American soldier with a grenade, or if it was an old and feeble prisoner from Afghanistan who had tuberculosis and was going to die in GTMO, he looked at them all the same: 'F***ing towel-heads'.

Offensive barbs like that always made me chafe. Parks would use other racial and ethnic slurs, and not just in the company of other soldiers outside the camp, but to the prisoners' faces. How could the prisoners not be justified in thinking that this was what America represented, that this was America's best and brightest? He was the type of guard who was out to 'get one' for America—to get payback for 9/11—to show them who ruled the world. This mentality was clearly shared by many guards at GTMO, but Parks had taken it to a new level.

Whenever an ERF was going to take place he was the first one in line and ready, even if it was on the other side of the camp. It would be the only time he would move quickly and with a purpose while hung-over, because he was going to "stick it to them". He would be the first to run into a cell, without the riot shield typically employed. He would run in, bare knuckles blazing, with a wild scream or a "YEEE HAAAAWWW RAG HEAD!!"

Even more disturbing was that Sgt. Parks had clearly fused with his ego, excising his guilt or indulging some other twisted conceit. His conduct was not in the best interests of the mission, the Army or his country. As for me, I stuck to what was decent, doing my job the best I could and conducting myself professionally, for America, the Army and the detainees. Yet I was held as a traitor.

This message of moderation and professionalism was impossible to integrate in the minds of the prisoners with someone like Parks around. And now he, of all people, was going to be directly over me.

The thought shadowed me the whole time I was home. I could not escape the stalking fear inside me. Just the thought of that cretin being in control of me was horrific.

Waking on the morning of my departure to Arizona, I forced myself to get excited about leaving. I was leaving that awful place and going home for a break. I hoped that the loving arms of my wife would be waiting, and that her scent would wash away the stink of rust and blood. I grabbed my stuff and walked out the door to board the bus and then the plane that would take me home. I even allowed myself to smile a little at the thought of being with my wife again. Starting to walk to the bus station, bag in hand, I ran into Sgt. Parks. The smile fell.

"You enjoy your time in the States, Private. When you get back, your a** is mine, and you're not going to be sympathizing with these terrorists anymore. We're going to scare you straight," Parks told me with a sadistic grin. When I tried to interrupt to speak up for myself, Parks continued with more ominous words. "You want to go join Al-Qaeda? That's fine, buddy. We will throw you in a cell with your friends and you can rot here with them too. I'm going to fix you, Private. You will love America again, and hate these Muslim pieces of s***! You understand me?"

What could I say in response? Words escaped me. I searched for a counter that would not bring up another belch of threats and cussing. This redneck, beer-loving, obtuse, card-holding member of the KKK was just waiting for an excuse. I changed the tone and thereby the conversation.

"Hey, Sergeant, I know you like Copenhagen and it's hard to get here. You want me to pick some up for you while I'm gone?" I replied, donning a plastic grin.

"Well damn-it private—that would be awful white of you. Pick me up a log—snuff, with the cardboard bottom," he requested. Now placated, Parks left and I proceeded to the bus stop.

How little Parks knew about my love of America. My desire to return to America was so strong it was the only thing keeping my chin up as I sat there, waiting for my ride home. I just knew that returning to American soil, to my home, would dispel the darkness that had wound itself around my heart, erasing my pain, renewing me and preparing me to return.

The Help of Allah

As anyone who has recently accepted Islam knows, not all goes well when spending time with non-Muslim family members. As nice as the visit home was, I ran into some difficulty with my wife, with whom I had not yet shared my conversion to Islam.

New security measures in place at the airport made for a frustrating start, as it was difficult to locate my wife circling the airport in her car. Denied access to the terminal without a ticket to fly, neither could she park her car outside the terminal, since both actions meant a potential security threat. I was nonetheless eventually able to locate her. I finally had the chance to look in her eyes and kiss her. I was finally back where I belonged, or rather, where I wanted to be.

I felt infinitely better the second we met and embraced one another. Her smell, her fragrance, was so softening to my heart. I drank in her scent and with every breath, trying to cleanse the arid desert of GTMO from my lungs. I was back where I wanted to be—in her arms—and we had two wonderful weeks ahead of us. I should have tried to process through the issues that had fomented between us while I was away, but I needed peace and happiness so intensely and naively felt there would be time for that later, when GTMO was behind me.

I was in peace, at least physically, now abstracted from Sgt. Parks, GTMO, the War on Terror or any miserable memory of the previous months. Her presence washed all that away, for a time.

We talked for a while, catching up on affairs that had, thankfully, nothing to do with the Army. Life, emotions, and experiences overflowed in conversation as we found ourselves at a Denny's restaurant. She was slightly surprised that I didn't get my usual: the 'Meat Lover's Skillet'. She otherwise ignored my irregular selection, and we continued on.

I immensely enjoyed the first two days. We talked a lot, held each other and reveled in one another's company, happy to be in love again. It was nice to spend time with her, doing simple things like cooking for her and telling her that everything would be okay. Compliments from her family were also soothing to my ears: 'You picked a winner', and 'Wow, he is a good catch!' Her family was unaware both of the trials we had faced and those still ahead of us.

Unavoidably, certain issues began arising on my third day home. The honeymoon was over that fast. The issues confronting us had only crystallized in my absence. They could be ignored or wished away no longer. My conversion to Islam was the least of those issues, but made me defensive, which is never a good place to begin sorting things out.

Naturally, she took notice when I'd go into the bedroom and lock the door for five minutes on regular intervals throughout the day.

"What are you doing in there when you lock yourself in?" she asked. It's like you're speaking some strange language."

Feeling awkward, I was immediately defensive and argued that she had been spying on me. This snowballed into other issues we needed to discuss, and ultimately ended up ruining what time we had left. It wasn't that I was afraid to talk with her about Islam. In other circumstances I would have delighted in educating her about Islam, about the huge gap between cultures and lifestyles unaddressed by our educations. I would have delighted in sharing my joy at finding Islam when I needed it most. I decided to avoid mentioning it because I feared being seen as a 'traitor', of 'switching sides', tainting the conversation. I figured that explaining my conversion would have to wait. Separation takes its toll on a marriage. There were many other things on our plates, so we needed to process our other issues first. Unfortunately, it didn't happen that way. Our 'sorting-out' proved more difficult than getting lesser things in order. Every issue we had was unpacked and exposed.

We argued for the greater part of the remainder of my leave, merely furthering our instability as nothing really had been resolved.

Delaying our issues for the fifteen-minute phone calls and emails wasn't the wisest choice, but what choice did I have in that situation? Alas, time waits for no one.

I needed time to shrug off the ominous, dark cloud of threats from Sgt. Parks, and his body odor never quite left my nostrils the entire time I was on leave. As often happens when spending time with the people you love, it was over too soon, and I was again packing. I was going back to GTMO, to the Regime, and to the very sergeant who wanted to fight me because he felt I was a traitor to America.

I picked up the Copenhagen for Parks, fear creeping back into my mind. I was upset by the state of my marriage, but fears about the future of my marriage gave way to fears of returning to GTMO, to a place under Parks. My wife and I said our goodbyes, and with a kiss on the head, off I went to that awful, miserable place.

I sat down on the plane, telling them who I was and where I was going, and drank the whole trip back to GTMO. Landing half-drunk, in a stupor, I felt ready for the hell that would be Parks as new team leader. I took my time getting back to my condo. I stopped in at the computer lab to converse with my wife one more time before things got awful. There was really no avoiding it, so, after a minimal amount of small talk, it was time to go find out what was in store for me.

I had prepared myself mentally for physical exhaustion due to excessive exercise, and braced myself for the upcoming mental and emotional denigrations and put-downs. I had assumed that a good amount of physical abuse would soon begin. Sgt. Parks, the 'good 'ol boy' who displayed the same joy killing animals as he did visiting strip clubs, was the embodiment of everything I loathed about the American South.

Under a stale cloud of dread, I walked from the computer lab to my condo and was stopped by my friend Bradley.

"Hey man, how was home, how is your wife? Have a good time?" he asked, oddly cheerful.

"Yeah, it was okay. Not too thrilled to be back now. I thought things were bad when I left...it's only about to become worse now, right?" I replied, miserable. The smile didn't leave Bradley's face.

"What are you talking about? Oh, you don't know! The Regime fell! First sergeant caught wind of what was going on and changed everything while you were gone," Bradley explained. The cloud dissipated. As the story of what had occurred in my absence unfolded, I learned that the drunken PT run, my black eye, and the fraternization that was commonplace had caught the attention of the first sergeant and our captain. They had changed the platoon structures, team and squad leaders, and put capable leaders in charge based on their ability level and not time-in-service. They took soldiers who should never have been on the island and had given them jobs where they had little or no interaction with the prisoners. Although the latter change meant more work for those who had been doing their jobs responsibly, it was nonetheless a vast improvement.

The best news was that Sgt. Parks was no longer my team leader. Now it was Sgt. Nord, whom I already knew to be more than capable, intelligent, and fair. When he introduced himself to me in the bearing of a team leader, his introduction confirmed my impression.

"I do not care what you believe, or who you side with, just do your job and do it right, and I will be your team leader and go to bat for you. I will help make you into a better soldier, and I will help you get promoted based on your abilities, not who you are friends with," he said to me.

What a blessing this new situation was for me! Allah had made my life easier, even though I had barely enough optimism left in my heart to hope for change. This was a far better return to GTMO than I could have anticipated. However, even in my newfound joy I didn't forget that I had a delivery to make.

I sought out Sgt. Parks. He still outranked me but it was clear that changes had been made and he had been seriously reprimanded. I walked up to give him his Copenhagen. He looked at me with a feeble smile on his face and simply said "thank-you." I could see in his eyes that first sergeant had really ripped into all of them. He had clearly put them in their places, and perhaps had opened their eyes to what being an American was really about. He may have even clarified what they were supposed to be doing at GTMO, as it was not what the Regime had been in the habit of doing. Allah had arranged it all while I wasn't even on the island, so I had no fear that the ex-Regime members would want to take it out on me. That I could not be fingered as the whistle-blower was an additional mercy from Allah. First sergeant had clearly figured it all out without the least of assistance from me.

This did not mean that I never had another problem in GTMO, as I was only half-way through my time there. However, I never again had a problem with the Regime after the first sergeant's involvement. The Regime—and the living hell they had created for those with a different world-view—had come to an end.

While Sergeants Parks and Johnsville didn't literally disappear, they were no longer in control of anything. They had been given jobs requiring little or no responsibility or human contact. Along with the other Regime members, they were assigned duties like working the radio for the DOC and escorting prisoners instead of being block sergeants; they were also placed on sally-ports, and left alone there. I didn't see them anymore, which was absolutely miraculous.

First sergeant must have realized that that kind of problem could fester and grow without his involvement, so his presence increased in company affairs during the workday. He began monitoring us at work every day, and inspecting the homes and the camps, making sure that everything was running as it should.

What I studied and how I spent my free time was also no longer under scrutiny. How I looked at the prisoners and how I treated them was no longer raising the eyebrows or the interests of those directly above me. I finally felt that I could be free to do my job well, and indulge in my intellectual pursuits at the same time with no fear of punishment.

After having been isolated and given all the work on the block under the Regime, my workload was now shared with a partner. My work partners observed my habits, and while some questioned what I was thinking (and whose side I was on) others just did the job with me. Others generally stopped looking at me as a traitor once team and squad leaders were no longer spreading lies and suspicions about me. At long last, my co-workers' evaluations were based on their own observations of my work, and I worked hard and well, which won me respect devoid of suspicion. I even started to talk more with the guards as time went by and I made a few more friends.

With the encouragement of my new team leader, Sgt. Nord, I began to excel in the military again, gaining rifle qualification and certification with my MP training. I even took a four-week course that would certify me as an official correctional officer. Nord kept his word, in that he did not judge me by my beliefs. He encouraged me to practice for promotion boards, and even worked with me on PT. Sometimes on our days off we would even hang out and play pool together, which was incredible, and welcome.

My at-work stress level thus relaxed, I was able to spend more time than ever speaking with the prisoners about anything and everything. I branched out past the Tipton Trio, the Professor and the General, Mr. Hicks and Omar Khadr, and even past the Uighur prisoners who were enjoyable to speak with, forever playing jokes on the guards and fun to be around.

In fact, I began to speak with every prisoner. Word of my conversion to Islam had spread through the camp and the prisoners were more excited to talk with me than ever before. Each day I went to work I learned something new, met a new brother in Islam, and learned more about Islam (and the world) than I had known the day before.

However, having a partner at work made it more difficult for me to talk with the prisoners. Having a team leader who cared about me and my work (and who managed to keep an eye on me from near and far) also made it difficult. It felt that I had returned to the real Army again, not isolated within an organism as before. What I strove for, and the reason I had joined the military in the first place, lit up again in my heart and I improved at every turn. My dialogues with the prisoners were an essential part of that personal growth, so I adjusted to constraints in that opportunity window by valuing my night shifts.

I focused on taking care of my work quickly so I could spend the rest of my shift speaking with the prisoners. I brought up questions about what I had read in the Quran, and about the Companions of Prophet Muhammad. I began to talk more and more with Shaker Aamer, who was back in Camp 3 again. Shaker Aamer taught me one of the best forms of dawah without even knowing. He never told me how to be a Muslim, or that I was wrong in my thoughts about the world. He would merely challenge me to look deeper into my own thoughts and opinions about the world, politics, and history to see whether the ideas I had were my own, or those I had picked up from the news and other sources. Then he would encourage me to research certain issues and search on the internet to expand my worldview. I would then see more profoundly into issues whose dimensions I had not fully considered. Shaker Aamer demonstrated to me that it is far more effective to show others the pathway to walk through—to let them do it and to know for themselves the truth and grace of that path—than to pull or push them along.

The two of us would talk about our lives. Aamer learned just as much about me as I learned about him. We spoke of religion, history, politics, ethics, morals, education, the War on Terror and its failure and many other topics. He made a valuable contribution to my sanity while working in GTMO, as did Errachidi.

I especially enjoyed the Uighurs, as they liked to play around with the guards. One time I was taking the trash from one of them, and he grabbed my arm and made like he was going to pull me through the door, joking.

"Oh, look who let his guard down!" he said to me before letting me go.

It was one of the things that I could play along with that the other guards would not tolerate. I enjoyed this relationship with the prisoners because they knew that I would not overreact: they knew that I understood their intention.

Another Uighur brother had drawn intricate images of tiger prints and various objects. Pencils or pens were not allowed nor accessible to the prisoners, so I inquired how he had done so, fascinated at the artistry and amount of drawing that the prisoner had accomplished. The prisoner pointed to his sandal, which he had fashioned into a crayon of sorts, and smiled at me. It was a delight and also a stain on my heart that these men were so creative and resourceful yet they were so misunderstood and mistreated by most of the guards. However, I continued to do my job. I also began to make some changes that reflected my mercy towards my brothers in Islam.

Bathing is not a privilege: it is a necessity. Taking bathing away is not something that should be used as a form of punishment. I believed this to my core, and since GTMO already had a bad smell, it was ridiculous following orders to withhold water for bathing. Seven hundred and seventy-eight men who were not showering daily, living in an environment where they sweated all day, exposed to one hundred percent humidity while living in ninety-eight degree weather resulted in an awful smell. It also created a less hygienic environment for all involved. So I conveniently forgot to follow orders denying bathing times.

If a brother was not allowed to shower for his 'misconduct', I would take him anyway. If I was caught doing so, I would reply that it must have slipped my mind. Most of the other guards did not care that I did this and neither did my leadership. As long as the assigned tasks were done at the end of the shift, my leadership was satisfied. Small kindnesses like this were tokens that I treasured, however miniscule. I felt powerless to do anything more to make the lives of the prisoners that much less horrible. I searched for any means (that would go unnoticed) to offer the slightest assistance to my brothers as they struggled through each day at GTMO.

Another way I was able to show kindness was giving extra food when serving the meals. At GTMO, there was more than enough available. It bothered me immensely that extra food was being thrown away versus being given to the prisoners as a second helping. So when I could, I heaped food on their plates, offering it to the brothers instead of wasting it. Although I would have much preferred to be hosting them in my home in the U.S., I was sure that those who had a high metabolism or were more active appreciated the extra food. Seconds were not allowed at mealtimes, but I did not see any harm in feeding the prisoners well the first time around.

Another of these kindnesses was also helpful in getting things done in a timely manner, and a benefit to the prisoners. I adopted leaving off the cumbersome and painful shackles when moving the prisoners. Every time a prisoner had to leave his cell, whether for a moment or a long period of time, protocol was that he would be shackled. The shackles used were three-piece units comprised of a pair of handcuffs, foot-cuffs and a waist cuff that were all intertwined. It was time consuming to get it on, and time consuming to get it off. Some of the prisoners had medical conditions that would make this an even harder and lengthier process—and the cuffs were abrasive—especially for older prisoners. The process of shackling the prisoners for every little thing was redundant and unnecessary.

The fact is that GTMO is enclosed on an island fortified by mine fields with a perimeter that is monitored by infantry soldiers day and night. Camp Delta itself is inside GTMO, and each brother was in a camp within Camp Delta. So, if by some remote chance an escape were to happen, the escapee would have to escape his cell, then his block, then the camp of his block, then Camp Delta proper, before finally escaping the U.S.-controlled area that is GTMO. The use of shackles was not a realistic component of security in this context.

As regards its importance in terms of my own security, I had less reason than anyone to feel afraid of the prisoners. If any guard—not just me—refrained from being rude or abusive to the prisoners, then there was no need to worry about guard safety. Therefore, seven months into my work at GTMO, I stopped using the shackles unless a prisoner was leaving the block altogether. My coworkers saw this and knew what I was doing. Some would get angry, and then I would have to use the shackles. Others would leave me to do the work when they saw a prisoner unshackled, so that only I would potentially be in danger. Of course, there were never any incidents. Under such careful watch, I was amazed that I got away with all these allowances. It is likely that they were observed and ignored due to the small impact they had on overall operations.

When problems did come up (usually after interrogation when a prisoner was upset and reacting to how he had been treated) an ERF would be conducted. I avoided them like the plague. I either dragged my heels getting ready so that another guard arrived first, or I simply did not respond to the call. It was easy to avoid participating, since there were so many others who relished the experience. The ERFs disturbed me less after my acceptance of Islam; I had adjusted to the revulsion elicited in me by the ERFs since the days of my arrival. I abhorred and avoided the practice because I wouldn't participate in the aggression and abuses meted out by the other guards.

The recent changes in personnel made it easier for me to conduct myself as the kind of soldier I wanted to be. I hoped that I could live up to the example I had set for myself of how someone in the U.S. Army should behave. I found no conflict of interest inherent in being a Muslim and an Army soldier. Those around me, Muslim and non-Muslim, were appreciating that.

MP Mustafa

I had heard many foreign names while serving at GTMO. Some I recognized, such as Muhammad (the world's most common name) and a variation of it, Ahmed. The Uighur prisoners and others from outside the Arab countries had fascinating and strange-sounding names. Some of their names were too difficult for me to remember. It was often easier for me to simply refer to a prisoner as 'brother' rather than struggling to pronounce correctly his actual name. However, a large part of calling someone by name is one's intention in doing so; the prisoners began addressing me differently now that I had embraced Islam. At first they called me 'brother', and then 'Mustafa'.

Arabic, like other languages, has in its lexicon certain words whose meanings have no direct English equivalents, and 'Mustafa' is one of them. Simply translated, it means 'chosen'. In the Quran, Allah utilizes the root of this word when describing how He chose the Prophet Abraham (and his family), Prophets Adam, Noah, Moses, and Mary (mother of Prophet Jesus). The name 'Mustafa' is one of the names assigned to the Prophet Muhammad himself. I didn't know the status of the name, so I thought it quaint that they affixed an Arabic name to me.

Calling me guard or soldier had previously been their regular practice. Those familiar with me would address me by my name, once they saw that it didn't bother me at all. I liked the sound of the name 'Mustafa', and happily responded when the prisoners called to me or greeted me by it. In general, newly converted Muslims choose an Islamic name, signaling those in their community to refer to them as such, but my community had chosen mine for me. Thus named, I continued working, trying to make the best of the days I had remaining at GTMO.

They referred to another guard by a Muslim name as well, although he hadn't accepted Islam. Pvt. Enrique became 'Khalid' to them, likely not from literal vectors (eternal, immortal) and rather more an implicit historical reference to the Companion of the Prophet, whom Pvt. Enrique may have resembled in some aspect of his character or conduct. It demonstrates that while I was unique in my attitude towards the prisoners, there were others among my coworkers who had cultivated working relationships with the prisoners. Pvt. Enrique and I favored compassion over aggression; we were both delighted when the Regime fell.

Consistency in respecting the prisoners was made easier by the fact that many of the prisoners were not, as was often repeated, 'towel head dirt farmers', but very intelligent and eloquent individuals. For example, they could pass information between camps within moments. The game of 'broken telephone' for schoolchildren is amusing for its limitations, but would be boring for these prisoners. Their communication skills, clarity and cooperation made them into a veritable human fiber-optic cable for relaying news.

Many of the brothers were not only multi-lingual, but also held degrees in law, medicine, and psychology: these were educated men. Neither the majority of the guards nor the DOC could understand we were guarding men with superior educations. It made their patience, perseverance and resilience that much more amazing to me, in light of the hatred and obtuseness directed at them.

In an attempt to prevent the flow of communication among cellblocks, at one point the DOC had placed all those who spoke Arabic on one block and all those who spoke Pashto on another. Instead of additional punishment, this relocation served to improve the lives of the prisoners, as it was a type of reunion for them, seeing brothers they hadn't seen in some time. At every turn, the prisoners seemed to be finding delight and happiness, although for all intents and purposes, they should have been the most miserable.

.Many of these men had been rounded up and sold to the U.S. to justify an exchange of money. Flyers were printed and circulated in Pakistan and Afghanistan with an image of a bearded man free on one side, behind bars on the other side, and the promise of payment for those who could turn in a religious Muslim man to military authorities. Although the poverty forced on many in the world is astounding, it does not mitigate the suffering of their brothers in faith, for which those involved in these schemes were partly responsible. Some of those bearded men taken may have been religious leaders in their communities, and were sold out as a means of extinguishing their leadership. What is clear (and centrally relevant) among the reasoning or methods by which all those men later found themselves in GTMO, is that the Bush Administration found it convenient to create an enemy. If they couldn't produce the enemy they had fictionalized, then they would make an artifice. Factitious totems would be necessary to legitimize the billions being pumped into the War on Terror. The terrorized American public would need to be fed (like the satisfying end of a cops-and-robbers show), images of bad men now arrested, captive and suffering. The case would then be closed and the American public could return to being unafraid, for the moment. That scenario would be one thing if the prisoners at GTMO had actually been guilty. The vast majority of them, however, were not, and would later be released after the war-invoice had been delivered. My next assignment was to assist in returning several prisoners of these prisoners to their home countries.

We received word that our unit had been selected for a flight mission. We were going to escort some prisoners home, or to another prison located in their respective countries. It required more training, as this had not been addressed in our conversion course; it is possible that no one anticipated we would be doing such a thing. We spent a few days preparing for the mission, who would be guarding and who would be shackling, who would be searching and who would be escorting. Keeping things simple, each guard had just one job to perform.

Flying to Iraq, Afghanistan, Germany, and Turkey sounded exciting to me. The fact that a few ex-Regime members were coming along did not dampen my anticipation. Although I knew the flight would end with us returning to GTMO, I expected a great flight experience. As it turned out, the flight was nothing but loud, chilly and uncomfortable—in every way.

The prisoners all arrived on buses to board the plane where my team and I were waiting. Wearing denim jumpsuits, their heads masked entirely and their hands and feet shackled, the prisoners were herded onto the plane like cattle. One by one, they were shackled to the floor of the plane. I couldn't believe my eyes, and asked myself, *If something should happen, would we be expected to unshackle the prisoners before saving ourselves?* Approximately fifty prisoners boarded the plane, followed by the guards. The prisoners were seated and shackled to chairs in the center of the plane, while the guards sat on chairs across from them. The prisoners posed no threat to anyone, neither in word nor action. Despite this, they were further covered by goggles and earmuffs as an additional (and unnecessary) security measure. Although insulated from the cold temperatures in their jumpsuits, the guards were all noticeably uncomfortable. The earmuffs must have provided additional baffling protection from the roar of the engines to which the guards were fully exposed.

The plane was a huge B-52 with nothing in it other than a couple of portable bathrooms, and the chairs and benches on which we sat. My unit held no weapons, instructed only to use hand-to-hand combat if necessary. An Air Force contingent was riding above us all with guns that would take care of anything if things got out of hand. Prisoners accessed the bathrooms shackled, and the Air Force guns stayed pointed at the prisoners the whole time. Not surprisingly, nothing happened. The guards in my unit took turns sleeping and watching the prisoners. Sleeping was problematic due to the roar of the engines and the cold. I was happy to have something different to do, but found the amount of guards and the rest of the security measures excessive, as usual.

As well as a 15-hour flight in those conditions can go, we arrived in Iraq safe and sound. The plane was grounded for as long as it took to unload the prisoners, verify their identities, transfer custody and refuel. Military personnel were at each drop, waiting to receive the prisoners. Everything went according to plan. I noted that we were not going to see much of these countries, as I had originally been anticipating. Iraq and Afghanistan looked to me through the doors of the plane just like GTMO: desert and rocks, lacking much that could sustain life. Adjusting to the realization that I would not be seeing the world—not by any stretch—but would merely be delivering prisoners, my reward would be landing in the miserable, hot, dust of Guantanamo, Cuba.

Our last stop was Turkey. A surprising announcement came from our first sergeant.

"Well, soldiers, job well done. We are going to have some downtime here in Turkey for a while, a couple of days.

Feel free to get settled in, even leave the base if you like, just don't get captured or killed, hoo-aah!" he declared.

Surprised and delighted, I considered it amazing that I would be able to see Islamic culture firsthand, in its native context. Neither shackles nor uniforms adorned my brothers and sisters, just the daily culture of the Muslim community awaited me. Bradley and I unpacked our bags, secured our belongings, and then headed directly off the base. I took full advantage of this opportunity. I flagged a cab.

"Take me to the biggest masjid there is," I requested. Replying hastily that it would be one-hundred U.S. dollars, the cab driver took me to the Sabanci Mosque in Adana. I had never seen anything like it before. In my experience, no cathedral, church or synagogue could compare: it was exhilarating. I ran up the steps and in through the front door, watching what seemed like thousands of people praying in perfect unison.

Everyone I met was courteous and polite to me. The visit to Turkey was a life-changing experience, and it was all courtesy of the U.S. Army! If it was strange and unusual for them, seeing a soldier from the U.S. Army inside their mosque, the warmth and hospitality of the Turkish people won me over.

I delighted in mingling with the locals, talking with them and drinking Turkish coffee, shopping and eating original Middle Eastern food. As I was Muslim, I had an easier time blending in, which must have been an eye-opener for the other guards who ventured off base. The Muslims there were receptive to us all and treated us with the utmost graciousness. They did not care whether my unit was American, military, or (predominantly) Christian. My visit there reaffirmed that we were unjustly at war with these people; that Islam was not the enemy; that the agenda was all a charade perpetuated by money-hungry warmongers. I knew it again at the top of the steps at the mosque in Turkey, that nothing else had ever felt so right: not my marriage, not the Army—nothing else felt as right as Islam.

My short weekend in Turkey was just what I needed to sustain me for the rest of my time in GTMO. A few souvenirs in hand, it was time for my unit and I to pack up and get 'back to business'. I came back refreshed and ready to work again. I noted that some of the ex-Regime members who had accompanied our detail seemed different after this experience, less hostile.

I eagerly shared my story and experience with the prisoners. I felt great as I told and retold my story about my visit to Turkey. I felt as if I were spreading hope that they would one day soon be going home. In those last few months, things flowed more smoothly than ever before.

"Listen, I am going to open your cell door and you are going to walk to the shower," I would explain, "Don't stop and shake any hands on the way, just walk to the shower, and I will not shackle you." Sure enough, the prisoners would comply, and whether it was due to respect towards me, or from the desire to avoid the shackles, there was never an incident.

I also no longer cared about the shower times. If a prisoner needed a few more moments in the shower, then I let him stay in there. It wasn't going to ruin my day or anyone else's.

Most of the prisoners held at GTMO while I was working there have since been released. I didn't know it at the time, but suspected that the great majority of them would have to be released sooner than later due to their obvious innocence. Whatever fate befell each of them, I wanted them to remember me as a good soldier, a kind brother in Islam, as a good man. That men scattered throughout the world could possibly remember me in this way comforts me when I consider my compliance with the Bush Administration's agenda. I had a limited amount of time to present to them a different picture, as my time in GTMO was coming to an end.

Goodbye GTMO

Working at Guantanamo Bay Detention Facility was not a job that I can look back on and think, 'Those were good times'. Although I was happy to have spent time with the prisoners and happy, of course, to have accepted Islam, GTMO was a despairing environment. I shared with others in my unit a strong desire to leave. So, when the time came for us to prepare to leave the island and return to the U.S., my concern was for the prisoners: what would be their fate after I left, and would I ever see them again, as free men?

I wasn't realistically able to do much for them. I couldn't stand in the way of torture and abuse; I only made life a tiny bit more comfortable for them. I had no authority to stand up for them in any way, shape or form. I'd never been able to influence any other guards to adopt my concern and compassion for the prisoners. When I left, they would merely have one less guard who cared. My worrying was lessened by the attitude of the prisoners when they learned that I would be leaving soon.

Confident that one day they would get out, they shared their email addresses with me, so they could keep in touch with me. Smiling and sending me greetings, the prisoners said they would miss me, but not in desperate ways that would make me feel bad, just sincere well-wishes. I began to realize that I would miss them terribly: I had grown to be close friends with some of them; I would miss our fascinating conversations together. The prisoners took note that the year was coming to an end, and that meant that they would have to square with a new rotation of guards. Perhaps they even afforded themselves a little hope that they would meet some other American guard that would be sympathetic towards them, displaying the kindness I had.

The replacements for my unit arrived for their training in the two weeks' prior to our departure. My unit worked our way out of the camps and off the blocks as we showed the new guards the routines. Those tired and weary of the work had trained us, and we showed the same inattention to detail in our training of the new guards. A year of being a guard at GTMO changes one, for better or worse; in either case one has less concern for professionalism at the end of his or her assignment. Routine grew weary and complacency followed. The workdays dragged on to that of our final shifts, when 'soon, honey, soon' echoed through the phone lines back to the U.S.

The tension between my wife and I grew as each day atomized our relationship. We had never resolved our issues, as that kind of work is impossible over the phone, or via internet chat. While I was excited to go home, I was bracing myself for a whole new set of challenges once back in the States; that last week my wife and I didn't speak at all. We were saving our grievances for when I was stateside.

When our last week arrived, my unit was moved out of the camp and into transitional housing just before leaving. I had said my goodbyes to the brothers, and had my last conversations with them, hoping to indeed catch up again, and perhaps even meet them again, in kinder circumstances.

I sat back and pondered over the last year. I reflected on what I had learned, how I had changed, and the tests and changes I had yet to face upon my return to life in the U.S. I not only had more clarity about my mission, and the inner workings of the Army, but also about the entire world, and my place in it. The seed of an idea was planted in my heart which would guide my growth in the coming years; if I was powerless to help my caged brothers in Islam while at GTMO, I resolved I would sure as hell try when I got out of that horrible place.

I spent my last days exploring the island some more, and was restless, waiting to leave. I went to all the places that everyone had been, and some places where I didn't think anyone had been in decades. I spent time alone, too, which was important for my thought process. I had found a community of men there who understood my desire to learn and did what they could to quench my thirst for knowledge. I had finally found a team leader who did not consider me to be a traitor and encouraged me to excel. Would I find that type of community and support once I got home? Something told me I would not.

I never got to see inside Camp Iguana or Camp No. I never did find out who worked those facilities, or why it was that

I was never able to know. I could not create closure around some of what I had seen in GTMO, neither with what I had done, nor with what I had been unable to do. My time there simply ended. Then it was the plane home.

GTMO had certainly changed me. I had grown leaps and bounds from the fresh-faced, naïve and largely ignorant soldier that I had been arriving there a year ago. I felt as though I had aged ten years instead of just one. Finding my center in GTMO, I had found faith. Incredibly, I was now a Muslim.

I had seen things that I did not think our administration would ever do. I had seen practices that had caused me to rethink, profoundly, how some people can call themselves good Americans. I began on that flight home to reframe the context in which I had matured, and to re-evaluate it in my head. This time, I had more of the missing puzzle pieces, and more direction, more truth. I could see more clearly the lies and omissions in the newspapers and textbooks I had read, and the news reports I had viewed on TV.

I knew my life would go in a different direction when I arrived home. I didn't know if my life was going to be better or worse than it was in Cuba, but it would have to be different. My mind was so full of deep reflections that I don't recall any of the events of the flight home.

A parade ceremony awaited us when we got off the bus, which was nice, but seeing my wife again after so long was pure gold. The problems waiting for us were like a gathering storm cloud, but I just allowed myself to drink in her sweet presence. Time with her and being home again whisked from my awareness all thoughts of GTMO. Bradley and I were both excited to see our wives, and were both so happy to be home. It was only an hour after we got home that Bradley and I decided we were going out to dinner together with our wives. The two of us had been waiting to come home, our anticipation building interminably, yet within an hour we felt uncomfortable because we were not with our platoon. Our wives became fast friends, and our two families intertwined. My wife and I spent that first night holding each other and talking. In that moment we were happy to be together again. She spoke of how she had gone home to Phoenix for a while, and how she had built a patio onto our new house.

I spoke not one word about GTMO with her, or with my family. None of us did. The events at GTMO were a dark world away, and I wanted them to stay there. GTMO sat in a dark corner of my subconscious.

It was only a matter of time that it would show itself.

One evening I had gone to sleep far earlier than my wife. She came to bed, trying to be quiet and not disturb me. She had gotten over to the bed soundlessly, and was just pulling up the covers to get into bed. Sensing a presence in the room, I launched myself out of bed, punched her square in the face, and took an attack position without even having opened my eyes. She held her face and cried, less from the pain of the punch and more from the unexpected and hostile reaction. I tasted the bitter realization produced by the nightmare I had been experiencing. I rushed to her side, apologizing profusely. She accepted my apology, understanding it was due to the side effects of my recent work. However, the incident changed her towards me. Neither of us was comfortable, and sound sleep was impossible, that night and other nights following. That unease followed us throughout the day as well. Our interpersonal context grew tenser as she watched me move about, not knowing if other outbursts would occur. She had heard and read stories about this kind of behavior and was nervous. Her fears were realized when it occurred a second time. This new reason for tension between us compounded the many things that led to our eventual end.

Before I knew it, I was commonly working 12 to 16 hour days at work, and I was coming home tired and exhausted. Field training and long days of work started back up again. It never occurred to me that I could have sought out counseling or medical help for my anxiety. It is likely that she thought of it, but was afraid to bring it up. When the thought slipped its way back into my mind, it was just confusion. *Why was this happening?* Dressing my psychological wounds had become a preoccupation, so I stumbled through life unaware and numb to the feelings of others. When my wife experienced some medical problems, I barely acknowledged them. We just continued on, coiled like two springs, pretending like there was nothing wrong. My exhaustion after work was an easy excuse to avoid spending any energy in discussion. While not forgetting my faith, when the tension became unbearable I gave into drinking. I felt as though I had already lost whatever was important, and through the false courage of alcohol, was ready to take on life alone.

One thing I underestimated while at GTMO was the value of community, religiously speaking. Although bars and wire stood between us, I was part of the Muslim community in GTMO. I was all alone in Fort Leonard Wood, even though soldiers were all around me. I saw no point in reaching out to friends or family, as it would only serve to recognize or acknowledge the darkness of that environment. I felt sure that even my friends would begin to doubt my allegiance, and I didn't want to deal with that anymore. Bringing up GTMO only reminded me about what I'd witnessed there—which I had difficulty with—and of the Muslims there with which I'd formed such a close bond.

Most of the ex- Regime members were moved out of my unit, or out of the Army altogether. First sergeant obviously did not want them around anymore, for which I could not blame him. We received new platoon line-ups, new leaders, new soldiers and many promotions. This dynamic prevented anyone from taking notice (or caring too much) that I had become a Muslim. My fellow soldiers had their alcohol, their wives, their video games and everything else American. My new squad leader, SSG Stewart, was just as encouraging as Sgt. Nord had been; he placed me into a leadership position with soldiers under me, which was great. We were conducting the entire field training (semi-annual and annual training) we had missed while in Cuba. We had some rewards, such as going to 'Confidence Courses' (for training) and further field training in land navigation, vehicle maintenance, and weapons training.

The whole time, Stewart was investing time and effort into developing my leadership skills, and I in turn was doing the same for the soldiers under me. I was taught early on in the Army to learn the job above you, master it, and teach it to those under you. Shortly after my return, I had made the rank of specialist. Work became life, and time at home was a silent battlefield. My marriage dissolved entirely, and I was alone. Even with so many men around me, including some who were under my tutelage, I was alone.

All the ingredients were there for me to become a conscientious objector. However, standing up for what I thought was right would cost me everything: my career, my financial security and whatever else I valued. I am not a hero. I'm not a patriot, either. I feel I am a coward. A hero would have said, 'No more!', and a patriot would have said, 'This is wrong and we all know it!' A coward is one who goes along with the program.

GTMO was supposed to be a pillow deployment; it was supposed to be easy. If everyone had just left their hatred at home, it could have been easy. There were sandy beaches, scuba diving and paintball. We also had a movie theater and a skate park to amuse us, but so many just got drunk, drowning in their hatred.

I feel deep regret over participating in what happened at GTMO, and shame for the other black-sites America uses to detain innocents. I feel personally responsible for how the world now looks at Americans. I want to tell people that not all Americans are bad apples. I don't understand how or why those committing the abuses and atrocities I witnesses are allowed to do so, or what happened to their humanity.

My disgust with myself led to a series of troubling years, until I took about someone's suggestion to try self-therapy by finally speaking out. The minute I put myself out there, I got requests for interviews. I began making arrangements to speak to the media and was able to tell people about what life was really like inside GTMO, and what should now be done to erase this blight on the American soul: that those held there should all be sent home. This book is part of that delayed reaction, to let the world know the reality of GTMO, so that people can be clear of what it is, for what purpose it is used, and the kinds of individuals that were inside (and outside) the cages.

It was, in the end, not for nothing that I worked in GTMO for a year. I feel bad about GTMO because I wish I had been a whistleblower, taking an initiative to stop it, but Allah has

His plan, and we have our plan. I did meet again with the prisoners with whom I had made friends, when they were free men. I keep in touch with many of them to this day through email. The high and undeserved esteem in which they hold me is represented in the beautiful introduction to this book, written by Ahmed Errachidi, formerly GTMO's 'The General', who has also published his own account of his time in GTMO, entitled *The General: The ordinary man who challenged Guantanamo.*

My reluctance and reasons for not speaking out while at GTMO are now gone, so I am telling people what GTMO is really like. My hope is that my voice—and my message—will both be clear above the cacophony of the mainstream media. I hope that what is presented here might, at least, get some out there to reconsider their long-held views about these matters. I hope that the year I spent in GTMO—and my brothers' many years of trials there—may serve some useful purpose toward the important work of enlightening hearts and minds about these issues.

I may not be a patriot or a hero, but does that make me a traitor?

Glossary of Terms and Abbreviations

SGT: Sergeant

SSG: Staff Sergeant

SFC: Sergeant First Class

PFC: Private First Class

MOS: Military Occupational Specialty - your job

DOD: Department of Defense

ASVAB: Armed Services Vocational Aptitude Battery

FORSCOM: United States Army Forces Command

OPSEC: Operations Security

PT: Physical Training

MP: Military Police

COC: Chain of Command

SOP: Standard Operating Procedure

BDU: Battle Dress Uniform

OJT: On the Job Training

JIF: Joint interrogation forces

ERF: Extreme Reaction Force

DOC: Department of Corrections

KKK: Ku Klux Klan

ISO: Isolation

PX: Physical Recreation area

OC Spray: Oleoresin Capsicum, Pepper Spray

MRE: Meals ready to eat

Islamic terms:

Sujood: Prostration, as in prayer

Adhan: The call to prayer

Dawah: Calling those who are not Muslim to Islam through words or actions

Jumuah: Friday congregational prayers, which includes a sermon afterwards

Hadith: An authentic report of what the Prophet Muhammad said, did, or approved of

Ramadan: The ninth month of the Islamic calendar, in which observant Muslims fast from eating, drinking, sexual relations and bad behavior from sunrise to sunset.

Shahaadah: the testimony of faith, which is said in order to accept Islam.

Fajr: The earliest prayer in the day, performed before the sun rises.

Asalaamu Alaikum: The greeting of Muslims, meaning 'May peace be upon you."

References

Ahmed Errachidi's interrogation 'confession'

http://www.reprieve.org.uk/blog/2011_08_22_CSS_AhmedErr
achidi_Granta/

Democracy Now's interview with Erik Saar, military translator

http://www.democracynow.org/2005/5/4/inside_the_wire_a_
military_intelligence

Ruhal Ahmed's interview, detailing interrogation at GTMO:

www.youtube.com, "Interview Ruhal Ahmed Part 1" posted by
prospecttv.

Contact Information

For comments, questions, concerns, death threats, or bookings, please email traitorbook@gmail.com Be sure to include your name, address, and phone or email if applicable.

.

Made in the USA
San Bernardino, CA
19 September 2015